UNDERSTANDING
CLASSROOM LEARNING

UNDERSTANDING CLASSROOM LEARNING

Noel Entwistle

HODDER AND STOUGHTON
LONDON SYDNEY AUCKLAND TORONTO

Changing Perspectives in Education

Series Editor: Noel Entwistle, BSc, PhD

The Core Curriculum   Gordon Kirk
Improving Study Skills   Ian Selmes
Understanding Classroom Learning   Noel Entwistle
Research on Education   John Nisbet
Appraising Teacher Quality   John Wilson

ISBN 0 340 40736 0

First published 1987

Photoset by
Rowland Phototypesetting Ltd,
Bury St Edmunds, Suffolk.
Printed in Great Britain
for Hodder and Stoughton Educational,
a division of Hodder and Stoughton Ltd,
Mill Road, Dunton Green, Sevenoaks, Kent by
Biddles Ltd, Guildford and King's Lynn

Contents

The Series Editor and Author

Noel Entwistle is Bell Professor of Education at Edinburgh University and Director of the Godfrey Thomson Unit for Educational Research. Previously he was Professor of Educational Research at Lancaster University and editor of the *British Journal of Educational Psychology*. His main research interests are in the field of student learning and motivation, and he currently chairs the Innovation, Research and Development Committee of the Scottish Microelectronics in Education Committee.

Preface

This series examines changing perspectives on a variety of educational issues and practices. It seeks to make accessible to the teacher and administrator, as well as to students, the most recent thinking, research, and development work in those areas. In education, ideas are presented all too often in a one-sided fashion, using rhetoric to disguise the lack of serious thought or supportive evidence. This series seeks to provoke balanced discussion on current issues based on a careful analysis of the most recent relevant information and research evidence. It will also present ideas and theories which are of direct relevance to teachers and administrators, show how these ideas are currently being developed by research, and what implications they have for practice.

The intention is to place current issues and relevant theories critically in a historical context but only so as to emphasise the changes which have subsequently taken place and the choices which currently face us. Recent thinking is described in as non-technical a way as the topic allows, with the emphasis on presenting complex ideas thoroughly but palatably. Practical examples are used wherever possible to illustrate the theoretical ideas being presented, and so make the classroom and curricular applications more immediately apparent. Recognising the limited time teachers and administrators have, the series tries to cover each topic in a concise manner, indicating additional reading and providing references to more detailed information wherever appropriate.

This book brings to the teacher a summary of some of the most recent research on classroom learning. Essentially it is about the work of educational psychologists who have attempted to provide concepts and theories of learning for the teacher. In the past these ideas have often seemed remote from the practicalities of everyday teaching. More recently, however, research has been carried out in the classroom, as opposed to the laboratory, and ideas derived from this research are more directly useful to the teacher. To some extent this new research enables the earlier psychological research to be seen in a different light, and some of that research still provides useful descriptions and explanations of classroom learning.

In selecting material for inclusion in the book, the main criterion has been not complete coverage of recent developments in the psychology of learning, but the extent to which the concepts and ideas can be seen to relate to classroom realities and provide useful ways for teachers to think about their own experiences and their current situation. Psychologists develop concepts to explain human learning in general terms; teachers are interested only in a special type of learning which takes place in classrooms. Psychologists develop many competing theories and progressively refine the concepts used to describe learning. They recognise that these theories differ in their fertility – their ability to generate new ideas for further research. But the theories also differ in their pedagogical fertility, their ability to generate interesting implications for education, to stimulate new thinking among teachers.

In choosing the topics and themes to be included in this book an attempt has been made to identify key concepts and theories which are most likely to speak to the classroom experience of teachers. The central focus is, however, an attempt to portray learning from the learner's perspective and to explore the implications of that perspective for the teacher. This focus leads to a final chapter which presents a model of classroom learning in an attempt to bring together some of the otherwise disparate ideas. And that model can be applied to quite different philosophies of education. No single method of teaching or learning is being endorsed. The reader is encouraged throughout to examine the ideas critically and select what is most germane to his or her own situation.

Acknowledgments

The author has been greatly helped in preparing this book by Jane Moore who typed successive drafts with skill and patience.

The author and publishers would also like to thank the following for permission to reproduce the following material in this book:
The Falmer Press for the Figures on pp. 22 and 83; Cambridge University Press for the Figure on p. 41; Scottish Academic Press for the Table on p. 71; Routledge and Kegan Paul for the Table on p. 95; JAI Press for the Table on p. 113.

1

Contrasting Explanations of Learning

Psychology and the Teacher

What can psychology offer to the teacher? Teaching is a demanding profession requiring a range of skills and knowledge. The teacher has the responsibility of presenting information and ideas to pupils in ways which will help them to learn. At the same time the teacher is influencing the pupils' attitudes and values, often unconsciously. Moreover the teacher has considerable influence over the way pupils come to view the whole process of education, with effects which stretch well into adult life.

The teacher accumulates a wide range of experiences about classroom learning but it is necessarily subjective and anecdotal. There is rarely the time or the opportunity to systematise, or reflect on, that experience. Psychology, in contrast, is the systematic study of human behaviour and thinking processes. Its aim has been to uncover general laws which govern learning and behaviour. By systematically observing human behaviour under varying conditions, psychologists are able to describe and, to some extent, explain the conditions favourable to learning. They also have suggested ways of eliminating undesirable behaviour. Their aim is objective, scientific knowledge.

It is not surprising, therefore, that teachers have looked to psychology to provide guidelines to assist in the daunting tasks they face in the classroom. Psychological evidence should complement professional experience. But psychology is a new and relatively undeveloped science, and human behaviour is extremely complex. There was a time when psychologists seemed to believe that they had the answers – a general theory of learning which applied to animals and humans alike. Now psychologists are more cautious, and provide a variety of descriptions related to specific kinds of human learning – but what they say is more likely to ring true in terms of the classroom experiences of teachers.

Yet one of the difficulties teachers have had with psychological explanations of learning is that most psychologists have concentrated exclusively on the characteristics of the individual. Education, in contrast, is a social as well as a personal process. Learning, for the teacher, is inseparably linked to the classroom context. Experiments in laboratories are easy for the psychologists to control; they allow precise measurements which lend themselves to elaborate statistical analysis. But the theories developed from such analyses may tell us rather little about real life behaviour, and the help provided for teachers has been extremely limited. In carrying out their research on learning, psychologists have narrowed down their focus of interest, first to a manageable research problem, and then to particular methods of measurement and analysis. What is created is a precise but restricted view of learning. It is essential that psychologists should not then seek to impose such a narrow perspective, necessary for their own purposes, on teachers for whom a much broader view is a professional necessity.

There are other problems in using psychological research to inform classroom practice. If implications from the research are to be accepted by teachers and educationalists, they must be intelligible, plausible, and practicable. The language used, the evidence offered, and the interpretations of the evidence must be accessible to the teacher. In practice most of the research process is inaccessible.

Psychologists derive their concepts from theories which influence the way they label concepts. The labels are often chosen to signal their theoretical origins to colleagues, and they also must be precise and avoid any confusion with everyday words. As a result the terms chosen are often off-putting, even confusing, and can only be fully understood by those who are already familiar with the web of meanings developed in that theoretical area. In carrying out their research, psychologists develop tests or other instruments to measure the concepts. The instruments are designed and scored according to a set of technical rules. The evidence presented can thus only be properly interpreted by those who fully understand those technical rules. Finally, research psychologists are usually interested not in understanding individual pupils, but in discovering generalisable patterns of relationships between concepts. To discover these patterns they use complex statistical analyses. As a result, the research findings are, on all three counts, inaccessible to any teacher who has not taken an advanced course in educational psychology.

It was argued at one time that the solution to this dilemma was to explain psychological research procedures to student teachers. But given the short time available in initial training, and the competing knowledge demands from other areas, that solution proved impracticable. Effectively this means that the detailed research methods and evidence through which the theories are developed cannot be presented to teachers. Moreover, it means that it is pointless to expect teachers to use the whole vocabulary of technical terms being developed by psychologists. There are, however, some theories and some concepts whose validity is generally accepted by psychologists, which do translate into the educational context reasonably well, and which suggest plausible and practicable implications for the classroom.

This book provides a selection of ideas considered to have potential educational value. Detailed supportive evidence is not provided in justification of the ideas, although references indicate where the evidence may be found. The set of ideas is intended to indicate the variety of explanations of learning put forward by psychologists and how teachers may use at least some of these ideas to inform their classroom practice. The final chapter uses a sub-set of these concepts to develop a model intended to summarise the factors influencing classroom learning and to guide teachers' thinking about how these factors might interact within their own classrooms.

The aim of the book is thus to provide a survey of important ideas from psychology and educational research which have relevance to the teacher. Researchers bring to the study of learning their own preconceptions and their own experiences of learning and teaching. When they come to make sense of their data, their interpretations inevitably reflect those preconceptions and experiences. The reader is in a similar position. Some of the ideas will seem more attractive than others; some plausible, some far-fetched. It is important to reflect critically not just on the ideas, but also on your own reactions to those ideas.

Researchers are beginning to appreciate that education involves many different types of learning. Is your own conception of learning broad enough to encompass that variety? Rather than too readily accepting or rejecting the ideas presented, try to think of situations or educational purposes for which those ideas might be applicable, and then imagine how many of those situations might apply in your own classroom or in your own experiences of learning. If this book is to be more than a catalogue of inert information, the reader will have to play an active part in trying to relate the ideas to classroom realities.

This chapter outlines some of the earlier attempts of psychologists, mainly over the last 25 years, to make sense of human learning. It introduces a selection of important concepts and ideas, and shows how these ideas were used to explain pupils' success and failure and to make practical suggestions about classroom learning. Chapter 2 extends this discussion by looking at attempts at describing the structures and processes involved in human memory, and the implications these findings have for the ways in which we structure information and ideas for pupils. Although subsequent chapters will challenge some of the explanations presented in the early part of the book, it is still essential to understand what was said about basic learning processes and the way individuals differ in their capabilities to learn. The newer research builds on these earlier formulations.

The book can be seen as having two main organising principles. The first reflects the title: it presents changing perspectives with the later chapters mainly introducing the more recent ideas. The second principle is based on placing the learning theories into the broad categories shown in Figure 1.1. Some of the theories and theorists included in this table will be introduced in this chapter: others come in later chapters. This figure is intended to provide a framework, but it will only be fully understood once all the theorists have been introduced. It will thus be useful to refer back to this figure from time to time.

Figure 1.1 Learning theories, concepts, and applications

Type of theory	Theorists mentioned	In chapter	Associated techniques and concepts
Behaviourist	Skinner	1,4	Programmed learning and CAI
	Bloom	4	Mastery learning
	Bennett	4	Time on task
Information Processing/ Cognitive	Norman	2	Memory processes and stategies
	Ausubel	2	Advance organisers and concept maps
	Bruner	2	Spiral curriculum
	Resnick	4	Task analysis
Individual Differences	Gardner	1	Multiple intelligences
	Eysenck	1	Personality (Extraversion/ anxiety)
	Kozéki	1	Contrasting motivational domains
	Pask	3	Learning styles and pathologies
Interactionist	Cronbach	1	Aptitude-treatment interaction
	Entwistle	5	Heuristic model of school learning
Experiential	Marton	3	Approach to learning
	Covington	3	Self-esteem or self-concept
	Rogers	1	Encounter groups

Perhaps the simplest way of categorising the differences between the main theorists is to recognise that they differ in the degree and type of control envisaged for the teacher. Thus the implications deriving from behaviourist theories stress a high degree of teacher control. The teacher decides what is to be learned, specifies narrow behaviourally-defined objectives, writes instructional materials in line with the objectives, and uses systematic objective testing to ensure that the learning outcomes fulfil the defined objectives. At the other extreme, experiential theories stress 'freedom in learning'. The student takes control, under the guidance of a teacher who makes suggestions, provides a range of resource materials and encourages self-evaluation of progress. There is also encouragement to engage in collaborative learning and to express emotions freely.

These two extremes represent not just differing psychological theories derived from contrasting sets of data, but also contrasting philosophical positions on the nature of both man and education. At the top of the list, the ideas are closely related to industrial training, where required knowledge and skills can often be defined precisely. Towards the bottom, the ideas merge with the traditions of liberal education in which the broad intellectual and ethical development of the individual is paramount. Between these two extremes, psychologists have tried to see to what extent education can be systematically tailored to the characteristics of individual learners. The remainder of this chapter looks at these three main descriptions of learning which stress respectively the generality of the *principles of learning*, the *individual differences* in intelligence, personality and motivation which affect learning, and the ultimate *individuality in learning* shown by each pupil.

Principles of learning

Twenty years ago the dominant theories of learning were those of the behaviourists. Student teachers were required to learn in detail about the experiments of Pavlov, Watson, Thorndike, Hull, and, in particular, Skinner. Derived largely from experiments with animals, these researchers developed a narrow mechanistic view of learning, which was nevertheless extremely influential. Learning, it was argued, depended on establishing a firm connection between a stimulus (S) and a response (R). This group of researchers thus came to be known as S–R or stimulus–response theorists. Their concern was to improve the efficiency with which the required responses could consistently be evoked from an animal or an experimental subject. A series of important principles of learning were established, and are still accepted at least for certain kinds of learning.

The first principle is of *contiguity*. When a stimulus and response regularly occur in close succession they become associated and the stimulus begins automatically to trigger the response. Our own language is full of such associations. The word 'cat' is linked to 'mouse' or 'dog'. The first part of a well-known saying triggers off the remainder. 'Where there's life' . . . 'there's hope'. There are musical contiguities – the end of one track of an LP brings to mind the sounds with which the next track begins. And our everyday behaviour is full of chains of actions which are made automatic through repeated practice – whether it is getting breakfast or driving the car. Efficient everyday living depends on making automatic a great deal of what we have learned by frequent *repetition* which is the second major principle, the 'law of exercise'.

The third principle is called the 'law of effect' and reminds us that we are likely to repeat only what we find enjoyable, stimulating, or generally rewarding. Actions which lead to disappointment, anxiety, or pain will be avoided, if possible. A good deal of common-sense child-rearing depends on this principle. In early life children are content when they are warm, dry, and not hungry. Food is increasingly used to shape behaviour by making it a reward for approved behaviour. Later on it is followed by the use of 'privileges' like watching television, going out, or staying up late. But behaviour is controlled most commonly by verbal approval and disapproval. The parent indicates what is accepted, or 'right', and what is 'wrong' – and such consistent *reinforcement* with appropriate comments provides a mechanism which strongly controls the child's developing repertoire of behaviour. Thus reinforcement produces an association between the behaviour and an anticipated reward. But strong conditioning also limits the repertoire of behaviour in ways which may subsequently be seen to restrict the individual's range of behavioural and attitudinal options.

The final principle relates to Skinner's own research. He investigated the positioning of the reinforcement in relation to the S–R bond and showed how systematic schedules of reinforcement could be used to shape animals' behaviour. Thus a pigeon could be trained to walk in a figure of eight by gradually building up this 'unnatural' behaviour from its naturally occurring components. If the pigeon began to walk towards the right, for example, it would be given a pellet of food. If it subsequently went forward, a pellet was provided. Then if the pattern right, forward, left was followed, another pellet appeared, and so on until the full pattern of behaviour was shaped. From such experiments on animals, Skinner became convinced that efficient learning depended on:

1   breaking down what was to be learned into small steps, and ordering these into a logical sequence;
2   rewarding initially correct responses immediately, but using intermittant reinforcement thereafter; and
3   identifying relevant existing behaviour and progressively shaping it by reinforcement until it fitted the specified new behavioural pattern.

As these principles of learning became established, Skinner became convinced that all human behaviour could be explained in terms of these basic 'laws'. Learning in classrooms should be no exception. He therefore set out to improve teaching. The starting point had to be a careful analysis of the existing situation in terms of the experimentally verified principles of learning. Only in that way could we expect education to become more efficient. His analysis began as follows:

> There are certain questions which have to be answered in turning to the study of a new organism. What behaviour is to be set up? What reinforcers are at hand? What responses are available in embarking upon a program of progressive approximation which will lead to the final form of behaviour? How can reinforcements be most efficiently scheduled to maintain the behaviour in strength? (page 34)[40]

When Skinner had completed his analysis of learning in schools, he was appalled by what he found. Learning was not broken up into small 'chunks': pupils were required to learn substantial quantities of knowledge at a time. Feedback and reinforcement was not immediate, nor was it used systematically and progressively to build up the required behaviour. He came to the conclusion that teachers could never by themselves, shape behaviour effectively. It was impractical, in a class of 30, to provide appropriate reinforcement. It was essential to use a technique which ensured that children progressed by small steps and were given immediate feedback after each step. His solution was programmed learning within teaching machines.

To develop teaching programmes the teacher had to begin with clearly defined aims which were then broken down into behavioural objectives, the achievement of which could subsequently be tested. The topic was also broken down into small blocks which could ultimately become the 'frames' within the teaching machine. Pupils were generally required to fill in blanks in response to pre-prepared questions and their reward was to move on to the next frame.

Some areas of science and mathematics proved to be well suited to the technique of programmed learning, and some remarkable improvements in teaching efficiency were reported in the literature.[93] But before long, even some of the enthusiasts began to wonder what had caused the improvements. Was it the application of Skinner's principles – or was it the more careful analysis of objectives, and the time and thought put into preparing the learning material? Moreover, Skinner and his followers adopted a language and a philosophy which made the research more objective, but also depersonalised human learning and proved to be an impediment in persuading teachers to follow the precepts of behaviourism. It might be accurate within behaviourist principles to describe a teacher as a 'manipulator of learning', but such a description is unacceptable to most teachers who consider their role to be broader and less intrusive than this view implies.

One of Skinner's most influential articles, 'The science of learning and the art of teaching',[92] was written in 1954. His influence on psychology, for 20 years and beyond, was profound. Not until 1974 could another distinguished American psychologist, Wilbert McKeachie, announce 'The decline and fall of the laws of learning'.[40] McKeachie reviewed research on human learning and concluded that each of the main principles could be refuted, at least as a general truth. Reinforcement did not have to be immediate, repetition did not necessarily lead to effective learning, and even knowledge of results did not work in the straightforward way Skinner had described. McKeachie concluded:

> The research evidence, I believe, demonstrates that each point enunciated by Skinner is untrue – at least in as general a sense as he believed. This does not mean that Skinner's attempts to

influence education have been bad or that the principles are completely false; rather his attempt to make a systematic effort at application has revealed that what we psychologists once took to be the verities hold only under . . . highly controlled artificial conditions. It may well be that they also have applications in other restricted situations, but meaningful educational learning is both more robust and more complex . . . This complexity, so frustrating to those who wish to prescribe educational methods, is a reminder of the fascinating uniqueness of the learner (pages 48–9).[10]

This critique of Skinner's attempts to influence education should not be taken as a denial of the validity of the principles of contiguity, repetition and reinforcement through feedback and reward. These basic principles still have to be borne in mind. But learning in school is not directly analogous to the shaping of the behaviour patterns of animals. The learning we require of pupils is not the unconscious link between stimulus and response, but the acquisition of knowledge and skills which can be used reflectively and applied effectively in subsequent education and later life. There are, however, times when the teacher must think first about the basic principles of learning. Am I giving appropriate opportunities for practice (repetition), am I giving sufficient feedback about mistakes, or am I using praise and blame in effective ways? But the S–R psychology proved too simplistic to explain a wide range of human behaviour in social settings and too mechanistic to incorporate the individuality of human responses to stimuli.

Individual Differences in Learning

Psychologists generally accept the ultimate uniqueness of the individual, but they depend on regularities of behaviour to allow them to make general statements and to put forward, if not 'laws' then guidelines to assist teachers in understanding and so in fostering effective learning.

Ultimate uniqueness, in fact, does not rule out regularities.

Every man is in certain respects (a) like other men, (b) like some other men, and (c) like no other man (page 53).[60]

Skinner was seeking principles of learning where not only all humans were alike, but also all animals. The idea that people *differ* in the ways they learn or behave was not denied by Skinner, it was just this that was not what he was mainly interested in. Other psychologists, however, have made *group* similarities and differences their main concern, in a research area somewhat misleadingly described as the psychology of 'individual differences'. And the individual difference most frequently used to explain differences in school learning has been 'intelligence'.

Intelligence
It is an everyday 'fact' of a teacher's life that some pupils learn faster and more easily than others. The easiest explanation of that fact comes from using the idea of intellectual differences. Pupils differ widely in their levels of ability. This observation was confirmed by psychologists at the turn of the century. There were substantial and consistent differences in pupils' marks across different school subjects. Some pupils did consistently well, others consistently badly. And when carefully constructed psychological tests of reasoning ability were introduced, again pupils differed markedly and consistently in their scores. The concept which was introduced to explain the similarity in performance across a wide range of scholastic and psychological tests was 'intelligence'. And psychometrists have since been continuously attempting to refine their definitions, and their measurements, of intelligence.

The early intelligence tests developed by Binet in France consisted of a series of graded tasks chosen to be appropriate to a particular age. A child who completed most of the tasks at a particular age, for example, seven, could be said to have a mental age of seven. By contrasting mental age with chronological age, the relative intelligence of an individual could be assessed by their 'intelligence quotient' or IQ.

$$IQ = \frac{\text{mental age}}{\text{chronological age}} \times 100$$

The original purpose of Binet's work was to develop a way of deciding objectively which children were ineducable – and so could be excused the compulsory elementary education which had been introduced. The world wars provided another impetus to develop additional intelligence and aptitude tests. Very large numbers of recruits had to be assigned to appropriate roles within the armed forces. By the end of the Second World War the technology of psychological tests had been developed sufficiently for educational administrators to believe that such tests could be used to ensure a correct matching of pupils to the different types of school which had been introduced. In England and Wales the 1944 Education Act required that pupils should be educated according to their age, aptitude and ability, and the two- or three-tier structure of secondary education into grammar, technical, and 'modern' schools was introduced. Intelligence tests were part of the 'assessment batteries' used at age 11 or 12 to place children into appropriate schools, and into appropriate streams within schools. Once children were correctly placed at 11+, they could be left where they were. The evidence at that time indicated that intelligence test scores were fairly stable over a period of several years; indeed there was good reason to believe that intelligence was, to a large extent, an inherited characteristic. Separate educational tracks were thus considered to be psychologically and educationally justified. Streaming allowed teaching to be geared to the pace and style most appropriate to each different ability level.

This argument ignored the social factors which ultimately proved most influential in removing 11+ testing. But there was other psychological evidence already in existence which should have been taken more seriously by policy makers. Any measuring instrument has a built-in range of error. Readings from a ruler, for example, depend on the position of the eye, and even sophisticated instruments leave some uncertainty in the readings obtained. Tests of intelligence also have a built-in error. Instead of giving a pupil a label which stated IQ = 115, it would have been fairer to indicate the uncertainty associated with the measurements which would certainly have been 5 points, probably more. In other words, IQ = 115 + 5 (or in the range 110 to 120) was really all that could be stated with reasonable certainty. And that level of uncertainty would have made 'appropriate' allocation administratively very difficult.

Besides this acknowledged difficulty in obtaining accurate IQs, many psychologists became increasingly concerned about the narrowness of the definition of intelligence. For many years intelligence had been equated with the ability to carry out abstract logical reasoning. This emphasis restricted intelligence to 'convergent thinking' towards predetermined answers. What about the 'divergent thinking' which led to unanticipated, imaginative or creative responses? Were they not also 'intelligent'? And what about the whole range of aptitudes which people showed for particular subjects or occupations? Did they not count as components of intelligence? Over time the tests used by educational psychologists to assess an individual pupil's intelligence have come to reflect a broader definition. Thus the British Ability Scales, published by the NFER, contain six sub-scores – short-term memory; retrieval and application of knowledge; speed of information processing; reasoning; perceptual matching, and spatial imagery.

There continues to be a lively debate among psychologists about whether it makes sense to talk about 'general intellectual ability'. The continuing consistencies which people show across differing intellectual tasks, together with some links between IQ and both neurological differences (shown by electroencephalographic patterns) and inspection times (fast recognition of differences in what is seen or heard),[15] have led Eysenck,[45] among others,[26] to restate the case for the inheritance of general ability.

But few psychologists would now fail to stress that *measured* intelligence may change markedly over time where, say, a child's family circumstances change in important ways. There is also a recognition that, for certain purposes, it may be more helpful to distinguish different forms of intelligence. Howard Gardner,[52] for example, has put forward a theory of 'multiple intelligences' which may be particularly valuable to education.

He starts with a definition of intelligence which is appropriately broad:

> A human intellectual competence must entail a set of skills of problem solving [enabling the person] to *resolve genuine problems or difficulties* that he or she encounters and, when appropriate, to create an effective product – and must also entail the potential for *finding or creating problems* – thereby laying the groundwork for the acquisition of new knowledge (pages 60–1).[52]

Out of an analysis of a wide range of psychological, philosophical, and literary commentaries on the concept of intelligence, Gardner concluded that it was necessary to distinguish at least seven distinctive aspects of intelligence. He argued that these should guide both our measurement of intellectual abilities and our education of children. His initial list of 'multiple intelligences' included linguistic, musical, logical-mathematical, spatial, bodily-kinaesthetic and two personal intelligences. The last of these need some further explanation. Gardner sees personal intelligence as having two facets, one depending on a developing 'sense of self' and the other on the capacity to 'read' other people's intentions and feelings accurately in a social setting.

While other attempts to identify different types of ability have been derived from a particular psychological theory in isolation, Gardner's more broadly-based analysis produces abilities more recognisable in terms of school subjects or domains of knowledge. Gardner is, however, at pains to dissuade us from seeing these abilities as limiting; rather they provide *opportunities*:

> Multiple intelligence theory posits a small set of human intellectual potentials, perhaps as few as seven in number, of which all individuals are capable by virtue of their membership in the human species. Owing to heredity, early training, or, in all probability a consistent interaction of these factors, some individuals will develop certain intelligences far more than others; but every normal individual should develop each intelligence to some extent, given but a modest opportunity to do so (page 278).[52]

Again, although Gardner describes seven separate abilities, he stresses that, in reality, these abilities inevitably act in concert – their separation is no more than a way of clarifying our thinking about a confusing concept – 'intelligence':

> In normal human intercourse, one typically encounters complexes of intelligences functioning together smoothly, even seamlessly, in order to execute intricate human activities (page 279).[57]

Gardner sees opportunities, in the future, to provide intellectual profiles for teachers as a way of facilitating a more appropriate matching between the teaching methods and a student's abilities. He believes that because his 'multiple intelligences' are closer to recognised domains of knowledge, and because there are several of them, it will become realistic to carry out such matching. He also anticipates that children will follow different 'developmental tracks' along each intelligence, and that schools should provide a wide range of 'enrichment activities' to facilitate development along those different tracks.[53] But the applications Gardner envisages for his theory are still speculative. The 'multiple intelligences' have yet to be measured, and when they are, there may still be such a high level of intercorrelation that 'general ability' re-emerges yet again as the most effective way of describing 'intelligence', at least for some purposes.

Gardner's theory has been discussed at some length only to indicate the way research is progressing. It should serve as an antidote to those who argue that the concept of intelligence necessarily puts limitations on teachers' expectations – and thus should be banished from their vocabulary. How to take account of major intellectual differences in selecting appropriate methods of teaching, whether by grouping or individualising, is a recurring issue for psychologists and educationalists to face up to. And even the earlier limited definitions of 'general intelligence' have been repeatedly shown to 'explain' a good deal of the variation in school attainment between pupils.[26] It is not a concept to be spurned, although it is essential not to seize on it too readily to 'explain away' pupils' limited achievements. Intelligence is one of many factors which, taken together, help us to understand differences in attainment.

Personality

While intelligence is an important concept in explaining learning, it reflects only one way of differentiating between people. In everyday life we use a wide range of adjectives to describe the people we meet. Some terms describe physical attributes – they are tall or well-built: other terms describe psychological attributes – they are sociable, optimistic, or nervous. These psychological attributes represent our way of indicating differences in personality. Our experience is that people behave relatively consistently. We know what to expect – up to a point. Psychologists have tried to determine which of the multitudinous terms have the greatest explanatory value. Which concepts explain the most significant differences between people? And which aspects of personality affect learning?

Hans Eysenck and Raymond Cattell are influential psychologists who have investigated individual differences and have developed ways of describing and measuring aspects of human personality. They both consider it to be possible to describe personality in terms of a relatively small number of personality traits – dimensions on which people differ most markedly. Neither psychologist would argue that these traits provide a total description of a person's individuality, but the traits are helpful in investigating fairly consistent patterns of behaviour which are typically different between groups of people sharing the same personality characteristics. Although their terminologies and methodologies differ, the main traits identified by the two researchers overlap to a reassuring extent. It seems that five of the most noticeable personality traits are extraversion, anxiety or emotional instability, radicalism, tender-mindedness and conscientiousness.[35] The first two of these represent traits commonly used in everyday language to describe differences between people. Eysenck provides pen-pictures of typical extraverts and introverts:

> [The typical extravert is] sociable, likes parties, has many friends, needs to have people to talk to, and does not like studying by himself. He craves excitement, takes chances, often sticks his neck out, acts on the spur of the moment, and is generally an impulsive individual . . . The typical introvert, on the other hand, is a quiet retiring sort of person, introspective, fond of books rather than people; he is reserved and distant except with intimate friends. He tends to plan ahead, 'looks before he leaps', and distrusts the impulse of the minute (pages 59–60).[44]

Cattell and Eysenck have both used questionnaires or inventories to assess the strength of the main personality traits. The inventories consist of sets of questions carefully selected to cover the range of actions typical of people with that personality characteristic. A statistical technique called 'factor analysis' is then used to see how closely the questions hang together in measuring each trait, and after repeated trial versions, the published inventory is produced. The individual questions may seem to be unlikely to assess anything as complex as personality:

'Can you put your thoughts into words quickly?'
'Are you mostly quiet when you are with other people?'

'Are you an irritable person?'
'Are you troubled by feelings of inferiority?'

Yet when people have answered 20 or more such questions related to a particular trait, the picture that is built up (from the number of items answered in a consistent way) does produce a reasonably reliable assessment of group differences and some indication of an individual's personality.

It should not be expected that such personality profiles can provide a fully adequate description of human personality, nor could it be accepted that a person's behaviour would be wholly consistent across a wide range of different situations, yet it does seem that research using personality inventories can add to our understanding of differences in classroom learning. Certainly extraversion and anxiety have been shown to affect school attainment, although not in any straightforward way.

Early research on the relationships between personality and school attainment were based on the prediction that pupils who were introverts with a moderate level of anxiety would be the most successful. Too little anxiety, or too much, was expected to be deleterious. The research evidence is in fact difficult to interpret.[36] In primary schools, on the whole, extraverts seem to be more successful. In secondary school, extraverted girls but introverted boys do well. By university level there is a small general advantage for introverts, but this seems to be mainly due to their better study habits. Extraverts who also have effective study methods and are well motivated obtain equally good degree results.[43] Anxiety does not seem to follow the predicted relationship. On the whole, the graph plotting performance against anxiety shows attainment falling consistently as anxiety levels rise.[39] There is, however, more recent evidence indicating that any attempt to describe general relationships between personality and attainment will be misleading because of the effects of differing teaching methods, as we shall see.

Aptitude-treatment interaction
In the 1950s two very separate psychological research traditions existed. The first, typified by Skinner, set up experimental tasks to investigate learning: the other investigated individual differences through surveys and psychometric testing. The experimentalists

examined general learning processes, ignoring individual variations, while those exploring individual differences took no account of the processes identified in the other tradition. This extraordinary myopia was pointed out by Lee Cronbach,[28] who believed that it would be possible to capitalise on the strengths of both methods in a way which would have important implications for education. He was concerned with matching teaching methods to the strengths of individual pupils. He considered that it would be possible to identify aptitudes, defined broadly to include any measurable stable individual differences, for which differing instructional methods would be differentially successful. His subsequent research endeavour came to be described as aptitude-treatment interaction.

A great deal of the early research focused on intellectual aptitudes, with rather disappointing results.[29] It appeared that the more intelligent pupils learned more effectively no matter what teaching methods were adopted. However, the most recent studies do suggest that there are some interesting differences. A leading American researcher, Richard Snow, comments:

[General] ability measures usually correlate positively with [attainment] measures following instruction because most instruction demands some degree of retrieval, reorganisation, elaboration, and construction of new [combinations of information]. The [high ability] learners perform assembly and control operations that low [ability] learners do not perform . . . [The implications for education suggest that] a set of alternative instructional treatments should be designed to vary in 'incompleteness'. For lower [ability] learners, the instructional treatment should be made explicit, direct, and structured in detail so as to provide the procedural knowledge as well as the conceptual knowledge such learners may not be able to provide for themselves . . . For higher [ability] learners, instructional treatment should be left relatively incomplete and unstructured so as to allow idiosyncratic exercise of procedural and conceptual knowledge . . . Direct training for low [ability] learners conducted in parallel with instructional treatment, should aim at the development of specified learning strategies and skills and their flexible adaptation to real learning problems . . . Direct instruction [and training] that attempts to be detailed and complete . . . interferes with high [ability] students not so much because it does not fit the components they have, but because it does not fit the personal organisations of components they have, or want to produce and exercise . . . High ability students are often better left to practice their own strategies (pages 371–3).[94]

PERSONALITY & LEARNING

When personality aptitudes are examined, much stronger interactions are sometimes found. One particular classroom study provides a clear example of an aptitude-treatment interaction. When primary school children were taught mathematics in contrasting ways – by a traditional didactic method and by discovery learning – the most effective method proved to depend on how anxious the individual pupil was. Anxious children learned more from direct teaching, whereas pupils low in anxiety benefited more from discovery learning. The researchers concluded that:

> Some, but by no means all, children remember more when they are 'set free' to learn. A teacher could plan to take advantage of the observed interaction by setting up exploratory situations in the classroom, but at the same time taking care to provide anxious pupils with the kind of support associated with more traditional teaching methods (pages 138–9).[101]

TEACHING

A more complex intereaction was also found when pupils were set to learn in pairs.[64] The crucial aptitude in this case was extraversion. Extraverts did not work at all well with introverts. In fact the most effective combinations proved to be those in which both pupils had a similar level of extraversion (or introversion) but differed in anxiety. It appeared as if the nervous energy of one child was more effectively channelled through the calming influence of the other.

Discussion methods, or simulation activities, are sure to favour the extravert, while independent desk-work will suit the introvert. But it is difficult to demonstrate these effects clearly, because the effectiveness of any teaching method depends crucially on the quality of the teacher, and because pupils vary simultaneously on several important different aptitudes. The research does, however, imply that we cannot expect to find any one teaching method which will be equally suitable for all pupils. This conclusion will be reinforced by research introduced later on.

Motivation and learning

Although the behaviourists showed no interest in the effects on learning of individual differences in intelligence or personality, they did recognise the necessity of adequate levels of 'drive' or 'motivation'. The behaviourists saw drive in terms of physiological variations in hunger, fear, or anxiety. They also recognised that reinforcement would only be effective if the reward was perceived as such by the learner. A food pellet, for example, would be rewarding only if the pigeon was reasonably hungry. Feedback of results would only reinforce pupils who wanted to improve their performance. But at this point the explanation ceases to be behaviourist. 'Wants' perhaps implies goals – an uncomfortable complication for the strict behaviourist. But the idea of differing needs and wants is comfortable to educationalists. In their experience human learning is often directed towards conscious goals, and differing levels of motivation often reflect differing purposes or expectations from the experience of schooling.

In parallel with the exploration of the effects of personality on school attainment, educational researchers were examining the effects of motivation. Here the findings were much more consistent than those on personality. Pupils or students with higher motivation do consistently better than those with lower motivation at all age levels, ability levels and, generally, in both formal and informal primary schools.[4,95]

At first, school motivation was seen as a single trait, but gradually it was recognised that there were different forms of motivation. An early distinction was between extrinsic motivation, in which the rewards were sought in marks or qualifications, and intrinsic motivation out of interest in the subject matter being learned. Then competence motivation was introduced – the satisfaction derived from doing something well. Achievement motivation described rewards from competitive success – the boost to self-confidence from doing something better than others. But alongside achievement motivation – or hope for success – came fear of failure, the fear of doing badly and being criticised, which pushes some pupils to work harder. This form of motivation is rooted in general anxiety and is at its strongest in competitive achievement situations.[10]

Most of the descriptions of school motivation describe rewards or punishments in cognitive terms, but recent research in Hungary by

Béla Kozéki[62] has sought to remind us that there are emotional and moral, as well as cognitive, sources of satisfaction in schooling. He also draws attention to the ways in which distinctive styles of motivation develop among children, at first as a result of contrasting child-rearing practices, and later dependent on experiences in school. Figure 1.2 summarises the ways in which Kozéki suggests parents and teachers affect pupils' motivation towards school.

The concept of motivation is used to explain the amount of effort put into different activities. Kozéki argues that it is essential to identify different types of motivation which reflect the contrasting emphases in rewards and punishments experienced by children in the home. Parents can control behaviour predominately by emotion – by showing love or anger. They can use explanations and so develop a cognitive emphasis. Or they can stress what is 'right and proper' – the moral dimension. Teachers, similarly, differ in the way they try to control behaviour in the classroom and in the types of reward they offer children. Again they may show more or less emotion, back up their control with little or considerable explanation, and may or may not stress 'standards' or moral considerations. Out of these differing sets of influences children begin to develop their own unconscious preferences for different forms of reward and so show contrasting motivational styles.

Whereas earlier theories implied that high levels of cognitive motivation would always be advantageous, Kozéki warns that the success they bring can be at the expense of an unbalanced personality. His three domains of motivation are affective, cognitive, and moral which indicate the forms of reward the individual finds most satisfying. People whose rewards are sought solely in the cognitive area may be seen as cold and aloof in their interpersonal relationships, and their ways of obtaining success may be amoral, if not immoral. Kozéki sees a combination of cognitive motivation with either affective or moral domains as balancing academic success through a more rounded personality. And he urges teachers to recognise their responsibility for the all-round development of pupils, not just their academic achievements.

Kozéki's work can be seen as firmly rooted in behaviourist principles, but also taking account of the importance of individual differences. Although it uses reinforcement as a basic explanation of a child's developing motivation and personality, the emphasis on

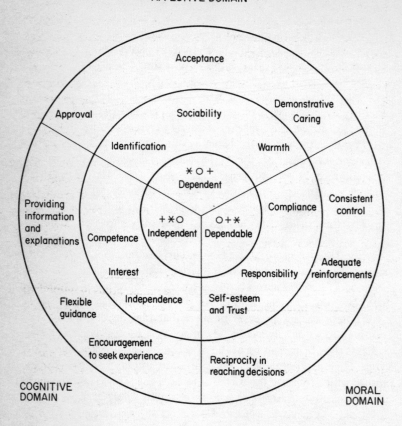

Figure 1.2 A model relating sources of motives to motivational style (from B. Kozéki (1985) 'Motives and motivational styles in education' in N. J. Entwistle (ed.) *New Directions in Educational Psychology – Learning and Teaching*, Falmer Press). *Key*: outer circle: behaviour of parents or teachers; inner circle: motives; and centre: most successful motivational styles.

morality and personal relationships breaks away from the mechanistic model of human learning, and brings us to experiential theories.

It is perhaps too easy to use concepts like 'motivation' to explain different levels of school achievement, and to assume that high motivation 'causes' high marks. To some extent that is true, but two important qualifications should be noted. First, most teachers will have experienced the motivating effect of high marks. If a pupil is given back work with an unexpectedly high mark, supported by encouraging comments from the teacher, the effect on that pupil's motivation may sometimes be quite dramatic. So high marks can cause increased motivation: the explanation does not flow just in one direction. And secondly, the level of motivation cannot be seen as a stable characteristic of the pupil. Motivation, and perhaps to a lesser extent the other individual differences, depend on the teacher and the learning environment. Pupils are often motivated by one teacher and not by another, and general levels of motivation are often a reflection of the ethos of the school as a whole. Again, this whole issue of who is responsible for the level and direction of a pupil's motivation will be discussed in later chapters.

In this section we have considered three main areas in individual differences – intelligence, personality and motivation. In later chapters we shall encounter additional ways of describing differences in the way people learn. The psychologists who have emphasised the importance of individual differences have not found a spokesman like Skinner to advocate a particular theory of teaching. But their influence has nevertheless been considerable. The original work on 'intelligence' led directly to the varying practices of 'grouping' – the attempt to tailor teaching to the needs of homogeneous groups of pupils by streaming or setting. Later the emphasis shifted to individualisation – the attempt to cater not for broadly defined groups based on IQ scores or examination results, but for the needs of the individual pupil described in terms of a range of contrasting 'aptitudes'. Was it possible to allow sufficient flexibility in teaching methods to provide ideal conditions for learning for each individual child?

The work on individual differences not only encouraged teachers to think about individualising instruction, it provided a range of concepts which teachers could use to try to understand why some pupils were not making good progress. Such understanding could then guide teachers to treat pupils individually, to provide the specific learning materials, support, advice or encouragement required to overcome difficulties in learning.

Individuality in Learning

So far success and failure in learning has been explained in terms of either the application of appropriate or inappropriate principles of learning, or the individual differences between learners in intelligence, personality, or motivation. Although the idea of differing goals and purposes has been introduced through Kozéki's model, it was totally excluded from the explanations of the behaviourists.

There was, however, a group of 'experiential' psychologists who bitterly attacked the inhumanity of both behaviourist and individual difference explanations which reduced the human being to either a bundle of stimulus-response reactions or a set of scores on tests or inventories. And the last thing either set of psychologists would have done was to ask not the 'experimental subject' but the *person* what it felt like to learn, what were the emotional experiences of learning, what were the reasons for learning. But that set of questions would bring back the explanations of success and failure in learning into the more normal discourse of everyday life, in which experiential psychologists believe such explanations can be most fruitfully and realistically couched.[56,86]

Carl Rogers was a psychotherapist who became interested in education. In psychotherapy, Rogers[85] had repeatedly recognised how personality disorders were bound up with a negative self-concept. If people were dissatisfied with themselves or pessimistic about their potential, they often retreated into apathy and disillusionment. Rogers found that if the therapist showed 'unconditional regard' for the client, growing self-confidence and self-regard often followed. Part of the treatment also involved the client in exploring and freely expressing feelings about experiences at home and at work. Rogers came to believe that personal experience had an immediacy and authenticity lacking in secondhand knowledge. Thus learning, or personal growth, depended both on creating a non-threatening climate in which the learner felt valued and on providing experiences to facilitate the expression and discussion of feelings.

Just as Skinner derived principles of learning from his experiments on animals, so Rogers used his experiences of counselling to develop a different set of learning principles. As we have seen, he was struck by the emotional components of learning, and by the effects of personal relationships on self-concept and confidence. Like Skinner, when he looked at what went on in schools he was bitterly critical of the experiences pupils were having:

> We frequently fail to realise that much of the material presented to students in the classroom has, for the student, the same perplexing, meaningless quality that the list of nonsense syllables has for us . . . Large portions of the curriculum are, for him, meaningless. Thus education becomes the futile attempt to learn material which has no personal meaning. Such learning involves the mind only. It is learning which takes place 'from the neck up'. It does not involve feelings or personal meanings; it has no relevance for the whole person . . . In contrast there is such a thing as significant, meaningful, experiential learning [which] has the quality of personal involvement . . . I believe that all teachers and educators prefer to facilitate this experiential and meaningful type of learning, rather than the nonsense-syllable type. Yet in the vast majority of our schools, at all educational levels, we are locked into a traditional and conventional approach which makes significant learning improbable if not impossible (pages 3–4).[86]

Rogers wanted the emphasis in schools to shift from teaching to learning. He encouraged teachers to become facilitators of learning rather than instructors, to show their feelings naturally, to be warm and responsive to pupils, to encourage rather than criticise, and to recognise that learning is most effective when it is both initiated and evaluated by the pupils themselves. This sounds idealistic and somewhat far-fetched, yet he provides a range of instances from childhood to adulthood in which the application of his ideas seems to have proved effective.

For example, Rogers cites the experience of one primary teacher who changed her teaching in line with his principles: she introduced pupil-centred teaching with an unstructured or non-directive approach. Pupils were initially allowed to do whatever they liked, and she found that many previously disinterested pupils came to life through their own enthusiasms. But she also found, as might have been anticipated from the research on personality and learning, that some pupils became anxious and confused by this entirely non-directive approach. Her changes introduced both the idea of a contract between pupil and teacher providing short-term goals to aim for, and a regrouping of pupils into those who thrived on independent learning and those who preferred more structure and guidance. Under these conditions:

> The children developed a working discipline that respected the individual need for isolation or quiet study, yet allowed pupil interaction. There was no need for passing of notes, or 'subversive' activity, no need to pretend you were busy or interested in a task, that in fact had no meaning to you. There was respect for meditation and contemplation as well as for overt productivity. There were opportunities to get to *know* one another – the children learned to communicate by *communicating* . . . Day to day one can sense the growth in communication . . . the difference in attitude, the increased interest, the growing pride in self-improvement . . . [This programme] is not *the* panacea, but it is a step forward. Each day is a new adventure; there are moments of stress, concern, pleasure – they are all stepping stones to our goal of self-actualisation (pages 19, 21).[36]

While Rogers repeatedly stressed the importance of changing the relationship between pupil and teacher, his ideas on education went much further. He believed that traditional education had become lop-sided. Rationality had been allowed to exclude from the classroom the power of emotionality; explanations had ousted feelings:

> A feeling is an emotionally tinged experience, together with its personal meaning. Thus it includes the emotion but also the cognitive content of the meaning of that emotion in its experiential context. They are experienced inseparably in the moment . . . the stress that recent centuries have placed upon reason, thinking, and rationality is the attempt to divorce two actually inseparable components of experience, to the detriment of our humanity.[87]

Rogers experimented with what he called 'encounter groups' to encourage adults and children alike to express both positive and negative feelings freely. In this technique small groups of people are invited to use leaderless discussions of their experiences to develop new insights into their feelings and their inner selves. A therapist may organise the groups, but Rogers sets the therapist as facilitator, not leader. This procedure has to be handled with great care due to the powerful feelings of hurt or inadequacy which are often brought into the open for the first time. But Rogers believes that, handled sensitively, this technique has great potential in education for both teachers and pupils. Many areas of our emotional experience are conventionally 'forbidden territory' in education, yet emotional blocks inhibit both teaching and learning.

The initial stages of leaderless discussion prove difficult for teachers and students. The conventional authority structure is overturned. But in time the group develops a dynamic of its own and facilitates, not just emotional readjustment, but also cognitive growth. An example from higher education illustrates the evolution of a leaderless group. The course had access to materials, but was given no lectures or formal seminars:

[Initially] the class didn't seem to get anywhere. Students spoke at random, saying whatever came into their heads. It all seemed chaotic, aimless, a waste of time . . . By the fifth session, something definite had happened . . . Students asked to be heard and wanted to be heard, and what before was a halting, stammering, self-conscious group became an interactive group, a brand-new cohesive unit. A student would start an interesting discussion, it would be taken up by a second; but a third student might take us away in another direction . . . of no interest to the class . . . But in this there was an expectancy, an alertness, an aliveness . . . as near [to] . . . life as one could get in the classroom . . . In the course of this process, I saw hard, inflexible, dogmatic persons . . . change in front of my eyes and become sympathetic, understanding and to a marked degree nonjudgemental . . . One might say that this appears to be essentially an emotional process. But . . . there was a great deal of intellectual content . . . [that] was meaningful and crucial to the person (pages 83, 85, 86).[87]

Leaderless discussion groups appeal particularly to Rogers because he is so concerned about transferring control and power from authority figures or bureaucracies to individuals. He wants teachers to become facilitators rather than remain instructors:

> The political implications of person-centred education are clear: the student retains his own power and control over himself; he shares in the responsible choices and decisions, the facilitator provides the climate for these aims. The growing, seeking person is the politically powerful force. This process of learning represents a revolutionary about-face from the politics of traditional education (page 74).[87]

Besides stressing the benefits of setting people free to learn, experiential psychologists also point out the importance of recognising the existence of contrasting perspectives of a situation, each of which can be seen as valid from the point of view of the differing participants. Thus, how a teacher sees the learning tasks presented in a classroom may be very different from the way they are seen by the pupils. And how a bright pupil views them will be different from a less able pupil.

'Encounter groups' have been used to help teachers become more able to empathise with pupils' learning difficulties. Guy Claxton illustrates the effectiveness of such techniques through the comments of a student-teacher who had been given the opportunity to reflect on her own feelings about learning in school:

> I feel more confident and run from difficult situations less often . . . I feel my own personal problems and my acceptance of them has led me to a much deeper understanding of others. As a teacher I have a feeling of empathy towards the children. I don't have to pretend to understand; because I do. I have felt what they feel (page 136).[24]

The essence of most of the experiential descriptions of learning is that teachers communicate effectively only when they are capable of the imaginative leap which allows them to feel what it is like to be the learner. The teacher then recognises the limitations in knowledge, experience, and self-confidence of the learner, and begins to teach accordingly. But Rogers is also presenting a radical view of education, reflecting a theory of learning which is also an egalitarian philosophy. It is in comparing the writings of Skinner and Rogers that the far-reaching implications of their ideas on learning can be seen. The whole nature of society is defined in contrasting ways, and the opposite roles given to the teacher are part of that total social philosophy.

Contrasting Explanations of Learning

When the teacher is faced with the apparent contradictions between the explanations of success and failure in learning provided by Skinners and Rogers, it is all too easy to dismiss the whole of psychology because of its failure to reach agreed conclusions. Yet it is important to recognise that all the explanations provided, be they behaviourist, psychometric, or humanistic, contain important and correct explanations of some aspects of certain kinds of learning. But they are also all *partial* in both senses of the word. Each theorist is focusing on a limited range of learning situations, and has collected a restricted range of evidence. Moreover the theoretical perspective adopted often seems to derive ultimately from personal experiences of learning. Jung once said that the difference between Freud's and Adler's theories could be explained by their differing personalities – Freud was extraverted and Adler introverted. Because psychology is the study of human behaviour and thinking, it is inevitable that each theory retains an element of subjectivity derived from the person's own individual experiences and beliefs.

The message to be taken into the following chapters is not that psychology has nothing to offer teachers because it cannot provide simple, agreed answers. It is unreasonable to demand simple explanations which apply to all people and every different learning situation. It should, however, be possible to see which ideas are of most value for particular educational objectives in certain classrooms or subject areas. The appropriate use and interpretation of the principles of learning then become part of the professional skill of the teacher.

In Chapter 3 we shall begin to explore ideas about learning which bring out the importance of the individual student's own goals and purposes in learning, while Chapter 4 explores the effects on learning of the tasks and instructions given by teachers. But in the next chapter it is necessary to extend the discussion on basic psychological concepts by looking at the educational implications of research on human memory and the ways in which we try to construct meaning out of our perceptions of the world around us.

Summary

Ideas about learning in classrooms have changed significantly over the years. In the 1950s psychologists believed that they had established principles of learning which applied to all animals, including humans. They described how stimulus-response associations were built up by contiguity, repetition and reinforcement. These principles remain true, but they are of limited value in trying to understand classroom learning.

Psychologists have also sought to explain the differing levels of pupils' achievements in terms of individual differences such as intelligence, personality and motivation. The definition of 'intelligence' has changed over the years, becoming broader through the introduction of several components: hence the idea of 'multiple intelligences'. It is also viewed as less limiting on potential achievement.

Personality also affects school attainment but not in the direct way once thought. There are potentially important interactions between pupil characteristics and teaching methods which warn against expecting any single approach being entirely suitable for all pupils. Motivation, however, consistently affects all level of academic performance, but here again it is viewed as enabling, rather than limiting. Children's motivation is directly influenced by parents, peers, and teachers.

Learning has to be seen as both cognitive and emotional in content. Teachers affect pupils' learning by the relationships they establish as well as by the information they present. There is an emotional component in learning which should not be overlooked: the classroom is a learning environment, not a knowledge factory.

The differing perspectives adopted by psychologists over the last 30 years represent alternative ways of trying to understand classroom learning. Some theorists view learning as under the control of the teacher; others regard the role of the teacher as facilitating learning. It is becoming clear that each theory describes only one aspect of learning, and is limited by the context in which the data was collected. Unless the evidence comes directly from the class-room context, it cannot be applied with any confidence to that context. The ideas from experiments or idealised learning situations may provide valuable insights, but these have ultimately to be tested in classroom environments.

2

Storing Information and Constructing Understanding

An important part of a teacher's everyday activities involves making judgements about how much pupils remember and understand about previous learning. These judgements often come in the shape of formal tests, examinations, or school reports, but they also take place every time a teacher answers a question or discusses a piece of work with a pupil. The teacher has to pitch explanations at a level which takes account of the previous knowledge of the pupil or the class, and sorting out difficulties often depends on reaching the bedrock of what is thoroughly understood and building up a firmer understanding of the new material from there.

Recent research is taking account of memory processes and the active role played by pupils in extracting meaning and developing understanding. One set of theories – *information processing* – examines different memory processes, while another – *constructivist* – emphasises the ways in which understanding is built up by reorganising previous ideas in the light of new information.

For one well-known North American educational psychologist, David Ausubel, effective teaching depends on rooting new material firmly into existing knowledge:

> If we had to reduce all of educational psychology to just a single principle, we would say this: 'Find out what the learner already knows and teach . . . accordingly.'[1]

Knowledge is stored in the memory; thus this chapter begins by examining what is currently known about the way we store and reorganise information presented to us.

Models of the Memory

There is a burgeoning literature in the field of cognitive psychology which outlines a fairly dependable picture of some important human memory processes. Inevitably a simplified description will not do justice to the most recent research, but a more detailed presentation would obscure the key concepts.

Psychologists have built up a variety of models describing the way humans process information. These models are mainly analogies based on parallels with mechanical systems or computers. It is extremely dangerous to accept these models as being descriptions of the way the mind actually works. All we can say at the moment is that it is *as if* it works in that way, but with further research a different analogy may prove to be more complete or accurate.

Information processing models of the memory, such as that developed by Donald Norman,[30] begin by examining our perceptions. When awake we are constantly bombarded with sense impressions which are consciously and unconsciously being interpreted. The range of impressions can be overwhelming, so selective perception is essential. We focus our attention on what seem to be the most useful or most interesting aspects of the incoming signals. This process generally involves consciously tuning in one sense at a time, and then narrowing our focus further until a limited set of perceptions from that sense is available for interpretation. For example, a child in the classroom might be feeling the hardness of the seat or the warmth of the sun, might hear the sounds of a group of children running down the corridor and what the teacher is saying, and might see what a friend is doing three desks away or notice a car passing the window. The teacher expects the pupil to tune out all the 'noise' of other perceptions and tune into the content of the lesson. In reality attention is rarely continuously fixed; it switches between perceptual modes and it varies in intensity. Impressions outside the primary focus of attention are not totally lost, but it is much more difficult to remember them subsequently because they have not been actively processed.

What happens when we process information? It is *as if* we have already in our memory a set of *schemata* or composite schematic images which represent systematised past experience. Thus a chair can be recognised visually from the way its component parts are organised. Its back, seat, and legs are connected in recognisable ways. A word, for example 'accommodation', is immediately recognised, *as if* we were comparing the word on the page with an image in our memory which also contains both the pattern of letters and its associated meaning. An individual schema also seems to have a range of other associations, more loosely attached, which is 'pulled up' from memory by that schema. Memory of a particular event may conjure up associated sounds, smells or feelings, and also similar events which happened at a different time. Perception, although generally automatic, is an active process in which incoming perceptions are matched to schemata. If the initial perceptions are not immediately identified, additional information is sought.[47]

Once the initial interpretation has been carried out, the sense impressions have been converted into a set of images which have at least potential meaning. Experience of everyday life is stored as a set of predominantly visual, auditory or kinaesthetic (movement) impressions (smell and touch are usually much less important). Not every event, however, is stored in a way which is readily retrieved. Again it depends on how much attention was paid to the associated sense impressions, and how much subsequent interpretive processing went on. But this memory for events or episodes (*episodic memory*) is extremely powerful and can be used to bolster other forms of memory.

Some of the information presented in class will be stored directly in memory without the need for further activity. Pupils vary enormously in their ability to absorb information in this way, but it is a capability which seems to be particularly strong during adolescence and young adulthood. Of course, this learning can only occur effectively if appropriate schemata are readily available and if attention is focused on the material being presented. It is, however, easy to forget how strong this capability is among young people – how else could they cope with the bewildering volume and variety of information which they meet lesson by lesson, particularly in secondary education. Some pupils have particularly powerful visual or acoustic episodic memories which allow them to recall verbatim their notes or even substantial parts of books they have read. Such 'photographic' memories are particularly valuable in examinations which test largely factual recall. But the examination results for such pupils will give no indication of understanding, and pupils who come to rely too much on this form of memory are likely to find the later stages of secondary schooling more difficult.

Photographic memories may also cause unexpected problems. For example, I once had to advise a student who had been accused of plagiarism in her course work. The tutor had given her a 'zero' mark because he believed she had copied substantial parts of the essay directly from a book. The student complained bitterly that the accusation was false – but the tutor was unconvinced. In the end of year examination, however, this student wrote answers which again contained substantial unattributed passages from books. Could that be plagiarism? Clearly the student's misdemeanour was not copying, but absorbing too readily what she read without reinterpreting the material to develop her own understanding of the topic.

Rote and Meaningful Learning

When pupils are asked to 'learn' something, the expectation is that rather more than focused attention will be required. Further active processing is expected, for which two main psychological processes are available. How do we remember an unfamiliar telephone number long enough to dial it? The number is repeated under our breath and held in *short-term memory* (STM) until the dialling is complete. However, if we are interrupted in some way, if someone asks us the time, for example, the number is likely to vanish. The short-term memory appears to be limited in size and duration. We seem to be able to hold up to a maximum of about nine 'bits' of information for up to about 20 seconds. The size limitation can however be circumvented by creating chunks of information, like a telephone number (081-367-1524) in which larger units are created and remembered. The *rehearsal* in short-term memory is acoustic and we use this repetitive procedure to commit to memory material which is either initially meaningless (like vocabulary lists) or which we have been instructed to remember verbatim (perhaps a poem).

Ausubel[1] describes this first process as *rote learning* and contrasts it with the other main process – *meaningful learning*. Schemata and images of past events are stored in long-term memory (LTM) which is essentially unlimited in size and duration. There are always large reservoirs of unused memory storage, and memory traces, once firmly established, last throughout life. Our memory lapses are failures in attention or in retrieval, not loss of memory. Besides the schemata of images, long-term memory contains *concepts* to provide a way of condensing meaning. A concept is a class of objects, (like a 'building'), or a general notion, (like 'freedom'), which can be defined formally in terms of its main attributes. In everyday life, however, a concept develops through the accumulation of experience of positive and negative instances. Our understanding of that concept is built up by seeing what fits or does not fit that particular label. Besides the episodic LTM, it is *as if* we also had a *semantic* LTM made up of the concepts we have developed. These concept schemata again have associated memory impressions which are brought together by thinking about the concept. Meaningful learning takes place when we try to make sense of new information or new concepts by creating links with our existing sets of concepts and factual knowledge, or with previous experience.

Young children automatically make sense of the world about them by building up schemata which include concepts. Even infants exhibit an apparent recognition of classes of objects, and the earliest function of language involves labelling objects in ways initially which emphasise their most obvious defining features. Thus 'moo-cow' and 'baa-lamb' are natural and necessary attempts at bringing together a semantic label with an acoustic defining feature. The process of language development involves finer and finer discrimination between similar concepts. To a baby, cats and dogs can cause confusion due to similarities in their visual defining features. But later on not only will these concepts become clearly separated, but different breeds of dog may produce more finely differentiated concepts. Of course, finer discriminations are only produced when previous categorisations prove ineffective, and when the discrimination is really needed.

Not only will every individual differ in the set of well defined concepts available, there may also be variations in the way each concept is understood. Effective communication depends on a high degree of overlap in the meaning of concepts, and this will occur with most concepts relating to everyday objects – table, chair, car, bicycle, and so on. But the degree of overlap in less common or in abstract concepts will sometimes be insufficient for effective communication. Ideas of 'justice', or 'democracy', or of 'education', are unlikely to coincide exactly. Our understanding will depend on the particular set of examples used to make the abstract sufficiently concrete or familiar to be understood. Technical terms in unfamiliar subject areas will feel imprecise or fuzzy through an insufficient set of examples or supporting information, even though they may be a part of our conversation. We may use terms such as 'volatile' or 'diffusion' correctly without understanding their technical meanings, but faced with a technical description of a chemical process the vague general meanings will not be sufficient to understand that process.

Understanding depends on the effective development and use of concepts. Education involves the use of increasingly abstract concepts, many of which may be defined formally. Such definitions can be learnt by rote, but then they are, in effect, separated in the memory from other potentially relevant concepts and experiences. Understanding depends on being able to develop a web of interconnections which relate previous knowledge and experience to the new information or ideas being presented. All too often it seems that knowledge in school is presented in ways which make it difficult for pupils to make the necessary connections, particularly with their own experiences in everyday life.

Douglas Barnes[3] explored teachers' use of language and concepts in a variety of school settings, and was concerned to discover how frequently the pupils' potentially valid experiences were excluded by the teachers' insistence on presenting information in formal ways which reflected their own sophisticated and abstract conceptualisation of the knowledge area. Why is it

. . . that children's existing knowledge is often excluded? The key to this lies in the way in which many teachers control both what is discussed, and how it is discussed.

Let us imagine a child who finds that his science teacher cuts him short when, in a lesson about light, he tries to tell an anecdote about shadows. To the teacher the anecdote is irrelevant: he has planned the work with beams of light and prisms in order to present to the pupils the physical principles which he has chosen to teach. For the learner, however, the shadows constitute his starting-point, the source of the understanding which he will bring to the prisms and beams of light. It is understanding of shadows which must be reconstituted to become a grasp of the physical principles. Thus what is irrelevant to the teacher may be very relevant to one of his pupils. The teacher makes decisions about which lines to pursue and which to leave, and these may often save wasted time. But if learners are always discouraged from utilising the understanding which they do possess, they will come to believe that school knowledge is esoteric and unrelated to the practical reasonableness of everyday action knowledge. They will then fail to use what they do know, and make wild guesses when asked a question. Moreover they are likely to under-value their own ability to think, since they have been shown that what they know already is valueless in school. Much teaching, especially in secondary schools, depends upon generating an artificial dependency in the learners, so that they can gain knowledge only by submitting to the teacher's view and not by thinking for themselves (pages 117–18).[3]

It is important to provide opportunities for pupils to use their own experiences, but it is also essential to help them to develop a more sophisticated conceptualisation of what is being learned. Often the *naive* conceptualisations drawn from everyday experience are inaccurate and misleading. They actively interfere with fuller understanding, and thus pupils have to be helped to reconceptualise their experience by having their current concepts challenged by new evidence which will not fit into their current understandings.

The gap between naive and formal concepts is particularly marked in science. Pupils often have erroneous explanations of everyday events rooted in their naive conceptualisation or alternative frameworks of understanding. Rosalind Driver[34] has drawn attention to this problem. She concludes:

It appears that alternative frameworks can persist in spite of instruction. Theories which are counterintuitive are not easily assimilated (or conversely, intuitions are not readily abandoned). In some cases quite profound changes are required in students' conceptualisations . . . If conceptual learning involves such major restructuring of ideas, then this has implications for instruction; we may need to pay as much attention to the learner's current ideas and how they change as we do to the structure of the knowledge to be taught (page 75).

Thus, while it is helpful to utilise pupils' experiences, it is essential also to establish firmly based, accurate concepts to facilitate academic progress in most school subjects.

A failure to have a firm understanding of the concepts fundamental to a school subject underlies much academic underachievement. Ausubel[1] believes that it is possible to identify key concepts or *anchoring ideas* in every topic, and that teachers should make sure that these concepts are very thoroughly taught, with plenty of examples, to form a firm basis for subsequent learning. Unfortunately, tests which emphasise factual recall will not provide adequate evidence of conceptual understanding. Many pupils cope with the tasks given by the teacher quite well *until* they are forced to think for themselves or display understanding. Ausubel argues that teachers have a duty to encourage pupils to adopt active meaningful learning, but his experience in schools suggests that, all too often, lessons are presented in ways which leave pupils relying on rote learning:

> One reason why pupils commonly develop a rote learning set in relation to potentially meaningful subject matter is because they learn from sad experience that substantively correct answers lacking in verbatim correspondence to what they have been taught receive no credit whatsoever from certain teachers. Another reason is that because of a generally high level of anxiety, . . . they lack confidence in their ability to learn meaningfully, and hence perceive no alternative to panic apart from rote learning (page 43).[1]

Advance Organisers and Concept Maps

Ausubel suggests that teachers can facilitate meaningful learning by using what he calls *advance organisers*. These are initial summaries presented in ways which provide frameworks linking together the concepts and relationships which are subsequently to be explained. Ausubel argues that having such a framework in advance helps pupils to see where the more detailed information fits later. By

drawing attention in advance to concepts and their interrelationships, it should also be clear to the pupils that meaningful
learning is required. Later on it is also helpful to discuss the
similarities and differences between what at first sight may seem to
be similar concepts. Such discussions show pupils how they themselves can try to develop finer discriminations and linkages among
concepts within their own cognitive structure.

Many pupils not only find difficulty in establishing firm basic
concepts, they also cannot see the links between sets of related
concepts. Joseph Novak[72] recommends the use of *concept maps* to
help pupils explore relationships. Figure 2.1 shows one such concept map describing the ecology of a rotten log observed on a field
trip. The concepts start from a central focus – log – and branch out
with the ovals containing progressively less central concepts. The
links between concepts are labelled to show the nature of the
relationships through *linking words*. Even with primary age children this technique seems to encourage meaningful learning and
deeper understanding, perhaps because it capitalises on our strong
visual memory for patterns.

> Whereas most humans have a notoriously poor memory for the
> recall of specific details, their capacity for recall of specific visual
> images is remarkable . . . Concept mapping has a potential for
> enlisting this human capacity for recognising patterns in images to
> facilitate learning and recall (page 28).[72]

Novak points out how a teacher can learn a good deal about a
pupil's understanding or misunderstanding through a careful examination and discussion of a concept map. The linking words and the
position of concepts in the hierarchical tree can be particularly
revealing. Pupils require practice before they use this technique
effectively, but even then the first attempt at a new concept map is
unlikely to be successful. Novak suggests that pupils should be
encouraged to make two versions: producing the second version
forces active consideration of the meaning of the linking words and
the positions of the concept ovals. A concept map can also be seen
as a powerful tool for emphasising anchoring ideas, within a structure which can act also as an advance organiser. Moreover, it
provides a way of assessing understanding as opposed to factual
recall.

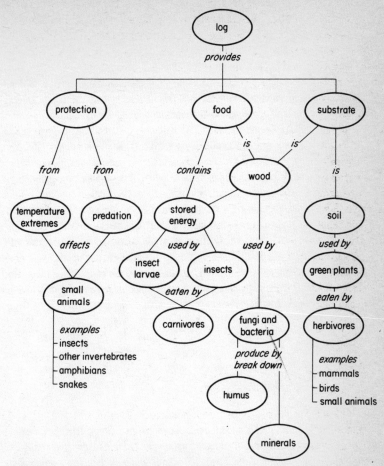

Figure 2.1 A concept map used to prepare an instructional unit, for fifth- and sixth-grade students, on a rotting log observed on a field trip (from J. D. Novak and D. B. Gowin (1984) *Learning How to Learn*, Cambridge University Press).

Retrieval and Metamemory

So far we have been stressing the structure of the memory and some of the fundamental processes used to embed new information and concepts in our memory. While factual information and rote learned material can be stored in forms which are identical between individuals, the attempt to reach understanding involves a transformation of the knowledge presented through the process of interrelating it to the individual's own network of semantic LTM. Gillian Cohen[25] comments:

> Although there is a common core of culturally shared knowledge, semantic memory is personal because each individual's knowledge and experience differs. It is not just a static mental encyclopaedia, but a working system, in which new facts are constantly being incorporated, stored knowledge is being updated and reclassified, and particular items of information are being sought, located, assembled and retrieved . . .
>
> Theories of human semantic memory are often based on computer systems for information storage and handling, but . . . [this] computational metaphor is misleading . . . While the information represented in a computer is, for the most part, detailed, precise and logical, human knowledge has quite different characteristics. Human knowledge is fuzzy, approximate and vague. A good deal of our knowledge is relational rather than quantitative. We may know that Leeds is north of London but not know by how many miles . . . Humans also have a mysterious faculty known as 'metamemory' . . . which enables us to know, with a fair degree of accuracy, what is in the store and what is not in the store, apparently without carrying out an exhaustive search (pages 18–19).[25]

In some models, the memory is likened to a large filing system[16] with each file being a schema or a concept. Incoming information has to be coded to indicate to which file it belongs and also cross-referenced with related files. 'Metamemory' can be seen as a filing clerk who has a general index. When a question comes in it is vetted first to see if it makes sense. 'What was Julius Caesar's telephone number?' would be immediately rejected as nonsensical: it would not lead to any search of the filing system. 'When was Julius Caesar born?' would pass the first test. The filing clerk then consults the index and may pass up the message that no exact information is available. How do we know that we don't know? The failure to answer such questions explains why Gillian Cohen called metamemory 'mysterious', but it is nevertheless an important part of our retrieval system. 'When did Julius Caesar die?' may again pass the initial review in metamemory, but now information is available. Perhaps there are linkages with Shakespeare which produce a two-stage answer: 'The Ides of March' followed by '15 March', but perhaps still without information about the precise year unless cross-references produce that answer from a 'history' area of memory. Alternatively, the date of Caesar's decease may not be found by a preliminary search, but the filing clerk may say 'I have the information somewhere, but I'm not sure where it is. I'll keep looking – go on with something else.' This feeling has been called the 'tip of the tongue' phenomenon, as the answer often 'pops up' later on when we are doing something else. It seems that our search processes are both conscious and unconscious, and it is important to utilise both strategies.

The filing-system metaphor is useful as it brings in the problems of retrieval. If information is not coded thoroughly, or if it is miscoded, it will be difficult to retrieve. Thus if we are to help pupils remember information, it is important to present material in a way which aids categorisation – in a clear structure and with advance organisers. It is also useful to help pupils to develop more effective coding procedures by discussing similarities and differences between the new information and established concepts or previous knowledge. And if pupils cannot subsequently remember the material, a teacher can help by providing prompts. Many pupils use their memories ineffectively. They need to be shown how to use search strategies which 'trigger' memory: too often they are simply reminded of the content. The importance of teaching about process as well as knowledge is a recurring theme in this book.

Thinking Processes and Intellectual Development

Education involves more than the effective storage and retrieval of information. It involves helping pupils to apply knowledge or to think things out for themselves. Such thinking necessitates the location of relevant pieces of information, examining their interrelationships, and then reorganising them appropriately. This process can be thought of as carried out in the *working memory*, which is an extension of STM utilising visual images and conceptual relationships as well as acoustic forms of memory. One function of working memory is to carry out mental operations on the raw materials extracted from memory.

Some of the mental operations available have been described in the section on 'intelligence' in the previous chapter. But the operations involved in thinking are not all available to young children: they develop only gradually during childhood and adolescence. The thinking of young children relies mainly on concrete operations, being dominated by everyday experience and intuition. Only gradually are children able to cope with abstract concepts and think in terms of more than one concept at a time. During adolescence the accepted forms of logical reasoning replace, or at least supplement, intuitive approaches to problem solving: these are described as 'formal operations'.

It was Jean Piaget who first set out the theory of discrete stages in intellectual development, and related these stages to typical age ranges.[79] His ideas were intended to show that children's thinking differs qualitatively from adult thinking. Although for many years Piaget's stages were taken as indicating limits to children's thinking, more recent research[33] has shown that even young children are capable of logical thinking and that pupils are likely to use formal operations on some occasions and concrete operations on others. It is thus misleading to describe children in terms of stages.

Although it is wrong to label individual children, it is possible to examine the difficulty level of topics to decide how appropriate they are for a particular age-group and ability level. Michael Shayer[91], for example, has argued from the results of Piagetian experiments that many of the topics included in the science syllabus of 16 year olds demand abstract conceptualisation and logical operations beyond the capabilities of all but the most able. Such analyses provide important warnings against the tendency to push into schools, topics previously introduced only at university level. There is, however, a problem in labelling topics as 'too difficult'. Is it that the topic or the concepts are intrinsically too difficult, or that the way they are presented is inappropriate to that age group? Jerome Bruner[18] has argued persuasively that developmental stages should be taken not as a limitation, but as a challenge. Teachers should try to find ways of presenting concepts and ideas to pupils which match their current thinking and encourage further intellectual development. His most controversial claim was that 'any subject can be taught effectively in some intellectually honest form to any child at any stage of development'. He was not suggesting that the details of complex academic topics, or the full range of the ideas involved in them, could be introduced to young children. Rather he wanted teachers to avoid underestimating pupils' abilities to reflect on important ideas if these had been presented in ways which matched the current stage of their thinking:

> There are ways of framing ideas that are appropriate to the level of development or abstraction that the child has reached. Lower levels of understanding are routes to higher-level ones. The lower level is not a degraded version of the higher. Each has a logic of its own. Each is to be respected (page 183).[21]

Bruner values the academic disciplines not simply as bodies of information and techniques, but as examples of contrasting ways of thinking and making sense of the world and human experience. Education is a way of making both information and ways of thinking available to the next generation. In his famous book, *The Process of Education*,[18] he argued that

> The great disciplines like physics or mathematics, or history, or dramatic forms in literature, were . . . less repositories of knowledge than of methods for the use of mind. They provided the structure that gave meaning to the particulars . . . The object of education was to get as swiftly as possible to that structure – to penetrate a subject, not to cover it. You did this by 'spiralling' into it: a first pass to get the intuitive sense of it, later passes over the same domain to go into it more deeply and more formally (pages 184–5).[21]

The idea of utilising stages of thinking through the 'spiral curriculum' is one of Bruner's continuing influences on educational thinking, but he also spoke out about what he saw as a failure of the schools to encourage deep, reflective, adventurous, and intuitive modes of thought:

> Mastery of the fundamental ideas of a field involves not only the grasping of general principles, but also the development of an attitude toward learning and inquiry, toward guessing and hunches, toward the possibility of solving problems on one's

own . . . To instil such attitudes by teaching requires . . . a sense of excitement about discovery – discovery of regularities of previously unrecognised relations and similarities between ideas, with a resulting sense of self-confidence in one's abilities . . . For if we do nothing else we should somehow give to children a respect for their own powers of thinking, for their power to generate good questions, to come up with interesting informed guesses . . . to make . . . study more rational, more amenable to the use of mind in the large rather than mere memorising (page 20;[18] page 96[19]).

Bruner put his ideas on education to the test by devising 'Man: a Course of Study'. This was both a syllabus and a set of resource materials designed to provoke thought and discussion. It incorporated his ideas on a spiral curriculum by revisiting themes with an increasingly detailed and abstract presentation according to the educational stage reached. Above all, he wanted intellectual activity:

We were all seized by the battle against passivity . . . it became a pedagogical style rather than a theory . . . I was worried that film, no matter how 'good', would sink children back in their seats and turn off their minds. How do you use film to get people to ask questions rather than accept the surface of things? . . . We kept the films silent. There was sound all right, but it was the wind or the cracking of the spring ice or the laughter and animated talk of an old . . . storyteller talking in Eskimo. But there was no commentator to take possession of your mind . . . The paramount value of the course, as one teacher put it to me, was that it posed problems in such a way that teacher and student both knew that they were together at the frontier of their thinking, brooding about the nature of man . . . [It helped] to cultivate doubt, to raise questions, to help the child see the world from another point of view (pages 192, 193, 195, 198).[21]

Modes and Styles of Thinking

The types of thinking that Bruner wants teachers to encourage can be seen to depend, in part, on the memory processes being used. The information processing model of the memory can also be used to draw attention to distinctively different modes and styles of thinking. Some of these are the 'formal operations' described by Piaget and involve the accepted forms of logical and analytic reasoning which have been used to measure 'general ability'. This process has also been called convergent thinking, because information from the memory is being processed towards a single product, a single correct answer. But there is another type of thinking, called variously divergent thinking, lateral thinking, or intuitive thinking. If convergent thinking is generally fast and narrowly focused, this other mode is broader and more leisurely. It explores an extensive set of features, not just the essentials, drawing on analogies and visual imagery, making connections with episodic as well as semantic aspects of memory. And this type of thinking is more personal and idiosyncratic than logical reasoning which uses set rules and the tightest possible definitions in reaching conclusions.

People differ not only in the content of their factual and conceptual memory stores, but also in their preferred modes and styles of thinking. The modes refer to the senses. Thus some people seem to rely more on visual memory, others on acoustic, and some on kinaesthetic memory. Everyone has all of these modes, but they often find one of these easier to use and so come to rely on it.

Similarly some people seem to prefer convergent to divergent thinking, and limit their thinking to facts and to cautious logical reasoning about convincing evidence. Other people prefer a looser, more intuitive way of thinking. Again, everyone is capable of both ways of thinking to some extent, but there are wide individual differences in the extent to which these have been developed. Even when both processes are well developed, personal preferences often remain. Where these preferences are strong and consistent, they can be called *cognitive styles*. In the following chapter similar preferences for tackling learning will be introduced and described as learning styles.

Although at least 19 different ways of describing cognitive style have been identified,[67] they all consist of two poles, such as convergent/divergent, reflective/impulsive, articulated/global. In contrast with 'intelligence', there is no 'high' or 'low' cognitive style. Each pole is 'high', but for a different purpose. Looking across the differing descriptions of cognitive style it appears as if they are describing differing aspects of one fundamental, underlying distinction (for example, convergent, reflective, and articulated compared with divergent, impulsive, and global), but what such basic dichotomy could there be in the mind?

The brain itself has in fact two distinct hemispheres linked by a bundle of nerves. Is there any reason to believe that differences in cognitive style could reflect preferential use of one or other hemisphere? Our left hemisphere is linked to the right side of the body and vice versa. It is clear that most people have consistent preferences for using one hand or the other, and therefore, necessarily, they have preferences for using one or other of the cerebral hemispheres, for at least that part of the brain which controls hand movements. But can this preference be extended to thinking? Do the left and right hemispheres process information in different ways? In her recent review of this question, Gillian Cohen[35] concludes that there *is* a specialisation of functions, although it is relative rather than absolute. There are differing descriptions of what these functions are, just as there are differing labels for the cognitive style dichotomies. Putting them together it appears that the left hemisphere is responsible for linguistic, symbolic, and semantic schemata, for conscious intentional memorising, and for logical, sequential, or analytic reasoning. The right hemisphere is used predominantly for visual, acoustic or kinaesthetic schemata, for passive, subconscious, or incidental memorisation, and for holistic or spatial reasoning. If there is this physiological basis underlying contrasting cognitive styles, it may be that it should be taken as much into account in teaching as children's left or right handedness.

One of the most eminent of researchers into the 'split brain', Roger Sperry, has not only reinforced the idea that the two hemispheres have different functions, but has presented evidence which suggests that the relative dominance of one or other hemisphere is genetically controlled. It appears that one gene determines the dominant hemisphere of the developing brain, while another relates to 'handedness'.

Sperry draws attention to the one-sidedness of education in schools which emphasises the verbal and symbolic thinking of the left hemisphere:

Our educational system and modern society generally . . . discriminates against one whole half of the brain. I refer, of course, to the non-verbal, non-mathematical minor hemisphere, which we find has its own perceptual, mechanical, and spatial mode of apprehension and reasoning. In our present school system, the minor hemisphere of the brain gets only the barest minimum of formal training (pages 58–9).[96]

There was a time, of course, when pupils in our elementary schools were forced to write with their right hand even if they were naturally left-handed. Now it seems the educational system is being accused of forcing pupils into left-hemisphere thinking. It is as if we are continuing to hit the knuckles of the right-brained thinker with the ruler of logical conformity instead of providing a choice between modes and styles of thinking within the formal educational system. The problem of coping with such diversity among learners will be considered later on. Now we can move on to how teachers can judge the quality of the products of these diverse ways of thinking.

Judging the Quality of Understanding

Our educational system is geared to judging, and reporting on, the quality of work produced by pupils. Even where this is not a component part of certification, it is still essential to provide feedback about what has been achieved and where improvements are needed. But our traditional approach to assessment has serious deficiencies. It uses norms to highlight differences between individual achievements and so fosters competitiveness rather than collaboration. In most subjects it assesses knowledge of facts, rather than the understanding of concepts and principles. And as part of its reliance on factual knowledge, it emphasises quantitative indications of achievement (marks or grades) more than qualitative judgements of the strengths and weaknesses. Of course, such a generalisation cannot be wholly true in every school and across every subject, but it represents a general tendency, nevertheless. Even in subjects, like English, where qualitative judgements are used, they may lack any justifiable rationale.

The previous sections have emphasised that only certain forms of knowledge are stored in the memory in ways which produce a uniform product. If our aim in education is to emphasise understanding, as well as factual knowledge, then we must accept, even welcome, qualitative differences in the ways pupils express their individual understandings. What they come to understand will be a product of idiosyncratic conceptualisation and modal and stylistic preferences in relating the schemata and concepts together.

In the past, psychological research on memory has concentrated on *reproduction* of learned material. If we are more interested in *reconstruction*, different ways of describing memory are required. Instead of describing it *quantitatively* in terms of how many of the pieces of information presented by the teacher can be retrieved to order by the pupil, it has to be described *qualitatively* in terms of the personal meaning generated by the pupils.

A qualitative approach to research on learning has been developed by Ference Marton and his colleagues at the University of Gothenburg in Sweden. They have examined differences in the types of understanding reflected in pupils' answers to questions about what they have learned. This description of the pupils' own experiences of learning has been called *phenomenography*. In Marton's research[65,66] a set of categories is produced which describes the main qualitative differences among the pupils' answers. These differences can be particularly revealing. For example:

[When Swedish pupils] aged between 13–16 were asked to give a physical explanation of seeing (i.e. of the fact that we can see an object in front of us), five qualitatively different ways of accounting for the fact that we can see things could be discerned:
A. The link between eyes and object is 'taken-for-granted', it is not [seen as a problem] – 'you can simply see'.
B. There is a picture going from the object to the eyes. When it reaches the eyes, we see.
C. There are beams coming out from the eyes. When they hit the object, we see.
D. There are beams going back and forth between the eyes and the object. The eyes send out beams which hit the object, return and tell the eyes about it.
E. The object reflects light and when it hits the eyes we can see the object (page 4).[65]

This technique allows us to map not only naive conceptualisations, but also the intervening stages before a fully acceptable physical explanation is reached.

While this technique provides valuable information about children's understanding, it would be impossible for teachers to explore every topic or skill for themselves. Are there any general guidelines which can be provided to help teachers recognise qualitatively different levels of understanding?

A starting point is a recent investigation by Alastair Pollitt and his colleagues of the answers 16 year olds gave to O grade questions in the Scottish Certificate of Education.[80] In what ways did the answers of the best candidates differ from those of the weaker ones? Of course the most obvious difference was in terms of factual accuracy and extent. The marking system coped well with this difference between candidates, but it did not cover other important differences in the quality of the answer. It did not differentiate between the answers in terms of the quality of thinking shown. It could be argued that such discrimination is not necessary in 16+ examinations. But that would also suggest that accurate regurgitation of rote-learned facts is a sufficient objective for the top half of the ability range – and that would be a curious admission. Although most of the questions demanded no more than description, what distinguished the best answers was an attempt to go from information to explanation. These pupils seemed to want to exhibit their understanding. They were dissatisfied with facts, preferring to go, in Bruner's words, 'beyond the information given'.[20] The need to describe these differences in the quality of thinking led to a search for a general scheme for categorising these differences.

An early attempt at developing such a scheme was reported by Edwin Peel and his co-workers.[78] Peel was interested in Piaget's stage of 'formal operations' and the ability to use hypothetical thinking with abstract concepts in different school subjects. He asked pupils to carry out tasks which demanded abstract conceptualisation and then categorised the answers in terms of the quality of thinking they showed. The main distinction which could be found across several school subjects was between *explanation* and *description*. Later these categories were extended into different types of explanation (extended and limited) and different levels of description. More recently Biggs and Collis[9] have developed these ideas further. They concluded that it was misleading to categorise *students* in terms of Piaget's stages. Even university students failed to use formal operations in answering questions on topics with which they lacked familiarity or interest. It did make sense, however, to categorise the *answers* to specific questions. This meant that the level of thinking could be assessed in relation to each piece of work.

Biggs and Collis have developed a classification scheme called SOLO (**S**tructure **o**f the **L**earning **O**utcome) to assess the quality of the work produced by pupils. There are five levels: prestructural, unistructural, multistructural, relational, and extended abstract. They describe, essentially, different ways of selecting and process-ing information from the memory. The question provides the stimulus. The student reviews the contents of memory and produces a response. A *prestructural* response is one in which the information produced is either a restatement of the question asked or irrelevant to it. In a *unistructural* response one piece of relevant information is presented, while a *multistructural* response contains several pieces of relevant information. However, in none of these first three levels of the SOLO taxonomy does thinking go beyond the selection of information and presenting it, where appropriate, as a description or a narrative. At the *relational* level, however, the relevant in-formation is interrelated and the conclusion is derived from that analysis. Finally, in an *extended abstract* response, the answer not only interrelates the information, but also brings in abstract con-cepts and theoretical ideas to provide a fuller, and more formal, explanation. Biggs and Collis illustrate these different levels through the answers to the question 'Why is the side of a mountain that faces the coast usually wetter than the side facing the interior?' This question was put to a class after a lesson on the formation of rain. The responses range from the clearly pre-structural (1–3), through unistructural (4) and multistructural (5), to relational (6) and an answer which draws on technical information way beyond the lesson to build up an advanced extended abstract response (7):

1 'Dunno.'

2 'Because it rains more on the coastal side.'

3 'Because when we go to our cabin that's right on the coast, it's always wetter there than on the road crossing the mountain that gets us there. Never fails, my Pop says. I reckon we ought to move; like get us a cabin for hunting which is better'n fishing anyway. Besides, I hate rain.'

4   'Because the sea breezes hit the coastal side of the mountain first.'

5   ''Cos air from the sea gets kinda damp, like fog and that. It settles on the coast first and so it rains and all the wetness falls on the coast and there's none left for the other side of the mountain.'

6   'Because the prevailing winds are from the sea which is why you call them sea breezes. They pick up moisture from the sea and as they meet the mountain they're forced up and get colder because it's colder the higher you get from sea level. This makes the moisture condense which forms rain on the side going up. By the time the winds cross the mountain they are dry.'

7   'This is likely to be true only if the prevailing winds are from the sea. When this is so, they pick up the water vapour evaporated from the sea which is carried to the mountain slopes where the damp air mass rises and cools. Cooling causes the water vapour to condense, and being heavier than air, the water droplets deposit as rain. Not only is the wind now drier, it is possible that it is carried up the mountain further where it is compressed, which warms it like a bicycle pump gets warm. It is therefore less saturated than before for two reasons. The effect is like the Chinooks experienced on the eastern slopes of the Rockies in Canada in winter. If there was no mountain, there would likely be no difference between the coast and inland. It all depends on the land features and the prevailing wind and temperature conditions. If these differed, then the energy exchanges would be different, resulting in quite a different pattern' (pages 4–6).[9]

The categories of the SOLO taxonomy illustrated above provide a way of taking into account the quality of thinking and levels of understanding, and the SOLO taxonomy has been applied to a wide range of school subjects. It is, however, important to recognise that the quality of the answers obtained depends to some extent on the way the question is asked.

The research on 16+ examinations mentioned earlier concluded that it was possible to control the difficulty level of examination questions by the format and wording of questions.[80] Open questions could be phrased in ways which demanded generalisations, abstractions, and a deep level of understanding. The same content area could, however, be examined in ways appropriate to lower ability levels by providing cues or information which guided pupils through the initial, difficult, task of 'decoding' the question.

A recurring theme in this chapter has been the importance in education of breaking away from an over-reliance on rote learning, and giving greater emphasis to meaningful learning and the development of personal understanding. Such a movement will also require assessment procedures which reflect the type of learning required of the pupils. But it is not intended to suggest that assessment should take account solely of these qualitative differences in understanding. Factual content and accuracy will still be important. At present, however, the balance tends to be so far towards the factual and the descriptive that pupils receive an insistent message that school learning involves no more than the accurate reproduction of factual information. As we shall see in the next chapter, such a message is likely to have a pervasive effect on the pupils' learning processes as well as on their ability to relate school learning to the realities of everyday life.

Summary

Models of the memory have been designed to categorise the different processes involved in interpreting, storing, and retrieving information. The memory has *schemata* or composite images which systematise important aspects of regularly experienced perceptual patterns. There are strong visual images of past events which make up *episodic* memory. But memorising in school makes use of *short-term memory* and the repetition or rehearsal of a few chunks of information. What is held in the memory by this method demands no interpretation and so has no personal meaning.

The *semantic long-term memory* is built up through the formation of concepts which have a meaning derived from repeated instances of those concepts. Concrete concepts will have a similar meaning to everyone, but abstract concepts have more idiosyncratic meanings and so are less easy to communicate. Where concepts are not firmly established, the meaning will be fuzzy. Pupils may fail to understand if teachers do not help pupils to relate abstract concepts to everyday experiences. Another problem, particularly in science, is that pupils may have firmly established naive concepts which are wrong. Then teachers have to help pupils to recognise the inadequacy of their interpretations of physical events before the more accurate conceptualisations can be built up. Advance organisers and concept maps are ways of helping pupils to relate new information to previous knowledge.

Remembering depends on appropriate coding of incoming information. Metamemory describes the capacity to know what we have stored without an elaborate search: it is as if we consult an index. Attempts to remember often involve using cues to bring back associations.

The mental operations used in interpreting the contents of the memory develop only gradually during childhood and adolescence. The information presented to pupils needs to be related to their current intellectual capabilities in ways which encourage active reprocessing of that information, not passive storage.

There are contrasting ways of searching memory which can be described as cognitive styles – cautious, logical reasoning as opposed to impulsive, intuitive thinking. These cognitive styles may reflect the differing functions of the two hemispheres of the brain.

The outcome of learning can be judged by the amount of information retrieved, but this ignores the importance of the quality of thinking involved. It is possible to classify different levels of answer in terms of the extent to which the information has been transformed by the learner. The SOLO taxonomy describes five levels – prestructural, unistructural, multistructural, relational, and extended abstract. Only the last two of these go beyond description to the point where the learner has demonstrated understanding.

3

Learning from the Pupil's Perspective

This book is about *changing perspectives*. It also describes how educational psychologists and educational researchers have tried to describe learning. As we have seen, their initial attempts were directed towards producing general principles of learning which would apply to animal as well as to human learning. The psychometricians were interested solely in human learning and looked for explanations of differences in learning in terms of intelligence and personality. Cognitive psychologists have also concentrated on human learning with a focus on how information is processed, stored and retrieved.

All these researchers have treated the activities of learning as happening to other people or even other organisms. What they have not done is to ask the learners themselves how they go about learning. One important shift in perspective in the research on classroom learning is the acceptance that it is important to understand learning from the pupils' perspective, which is different from those of both teachers and researchers.[37] A second important shift in perspective from the researchers is to realise that explanations of learning have to be related to specific environments. Whereas in the past it was assumed that it would be possible to investigate learning or memory in the laboratory, psychologists are increasingly accepting the need for *ecological validity*. They are recognising that concepts and theories can be valid only within a particular, defined environment.[69] With this realisation there has been a rapid growth in research into learning within the classroom and a recognition that any general ideas about learning may have to be reappraised in relation to school learning and even in relation to a variety of specific types of learning or tasks within the classroom.

As we saw in the first chapter, psychologists such as Carl Rogers saw the need for teachers to empathise with their students and to provide learning experiences which would facilitate 'real' learning. But Rogers developed his ideas and his techniques by extrapolation from his experiences as a psychotherapist. They were originally couched in terms of 'clients' and 'personal growth', and described the developing trust required between client and therapist. It is difficult to translate these ideas into the context of set syllabuses and classes of 30 pupils. Again such extrapolation loses ecological validity. We need to discover more about how students experience learning in classrooms.

An immediate problem in investigating learning from the student's perspective is that it requires the student to be capable of describing the salient experiences. With young children, such 'detached introspection' is rarely found. It is not surprising, therefore, that much of the initial work has been carried out in higher education. It is, however, becoming clear that the concepts and ideas developed from the introspections of university and college students can guide investigations of classroom learning. A second problem is that general questions to students about how they learn or how they conceive of learning produce vague answers which are difficult to interpret. It is essential to help the student to focus down from the abstract and general to the concrete and particular. Thus questions about how students are tackling or have tackled a specific assignment or problem produce more reliable and more interpretable descriptions.

Research on Student Learning

Approaches to learning

One of the main exponents of this method of research has been Ference Marton at the University of Gothenburg.[66] He was interested in how students went about the everyday task of reading an academic article. Although the students carried out the work individually in an experimental setting, the learning material was realistic and so were the instructions. 'Read the article and be ready to answer questions on it afterwards.' The students could take as much time as they needed and could make notes.

The first question they were asked was very general. 'Try to summarise the article in one or two sentences. In other words what is the author's intention?' After a series of more specific questions about the content, students were then asked how they had tackled the task – what they had been trying to do, what difficulties they had encountered, and so on. The responses were tape recorded, transcribed, and analysed. The researchers were interested in the processes students had used and how these processes related to the levels of understanding reached. The various processes mentioned were categorised and then grouped to bring together clusters of similar ways of tackling the task. In the end a single concept described two distinctive groupings – deep and surface *approaches to learning*. Perhaps the most crucial discovery, which in retrospect seems obvious, was that the processes used depended on the intentions of the student. Although it is obvious that intention will influence how the learning is carried out, it was not obvious in advance that students given the same instruction would interpret it so differently as to imply markedly different intentions.

With a *deep approach* the intention is to *understand* the meaning of the article. This intention generally leads to a lively interaction with the content of the article, relating it to previous knowledge, other topics, and personal experience. The evidence within the article is also examined carefully in relation to the author's conclusions, and often reassessed to produce alternative conclusions. If this approach is carried out thoroughly, and the student's previous knowledge of the topic is adequate, the outcome is almost inevitably a deep level of understanding shown by answers equivalent to 'relational' or 'extended abstract' in the SOLO taxonomy.

With a *surface approach* the intention is limited to completing the task requirements. Attention is switched from the author's meaning to the anticipated questions. The task is viewed as an external imposition devoid of personal meaning, and the student skates over the surface of the article seeking likely topics for questions. Once that information is identified, it is memorised by repetition and rote learning. The material is thus related only to the event of reading the article, and not to previous knowledge or personal experience.

If the student has a retentive memory, the relevant facts may be retained, but only limited factual answers can be provided – levels below the 'relational' in the SOLO taxonomy.

To make the distinction between deep and surface clearer, here are extracts from students' comments on how they tackled the task of reading the article:

> I read more slowly than usual, knowing I'd have to answer questions, but I didn't speculate on what sort of questions they'd be. I was looking for the argument and whatever points were used to illustrate it. I could not avoid relating the article to other things I'd read, past experience, and associations . . . [deep]

> Whilst reading the article, I took great care in trying to understand what the author was getting at, looking out for arguments, and facts which backed up the arguments . . . I found myself continually relating the article to personal experience, and thus facilitating an understanding of it . . . [deep]

> I stopped and thought about what they were actually saying . . . if there was something I thought wasn't right and so on. You also stop and then [wonder] if that really follows . . . is it really logical, what they've written . . . [deep]

> In reading the article I was looking out mainly for facts and examples. I read the article more carefully than I usually would, taking notes, knowing I was to answer questions about it. I thought the questions would be facts in the article . . . This did influence the way I read; I tried to memorise names, figures quoted, etc . . . [surface]

> You get distracted. You think 'I've got to remember this now'. And then you think so hard about having to remember it – that's why you don't remember it . . . [surface] (pages 40–1).[66]

At first sight the distinction between deep and surface may seem too simple. There must surely be many different approaches, not just two. This was certainly my own initial reaction. But then I asked a first-year tutorial group to read an article, following Marton's procedure. Going round the table asking them to describe the way they had tackled the task, each student clearly described either a deep or a surface approach. I was struck by how readily the

Table 3.1   Categories of approaches to learning

Deep Approach
   Intention to understand
   Vigorous interaction with content
   Relate new ideas to previous knowledge
   Relate concepts to everyday experience
   Relate evidence to conclusions
   Examine the logic of the argument

Surface Approach
   Intention to complete task requirements
   Memorise information needed for assessments
   Treat task as an external imposition
   Unreflectiveness about purpose or strategies
   Focus on discrete elements without integration
   Failure to distinguish principles from examples

Strategic Approach
   Intention to obtain highest possible grades
   Use previous exam papers to predict questions
   Be alert to cues about marking schemes
   Organise time and distribute effort to greatest effect
   Ensure conditions and materials for studying appropriate

---

approaches fell into one or other category. The students themselves were surprised at the very different ways they had gone about the reading of the article. When introduced to the concept of 'approach to learning', they recognised their own approach immediately from the defining characteristics (see Table 3.1).

It would be wrong to give the impression that a deep intention is always followed by the full range of deep processes. In fact very few students seem to use that full range. It seems that some concentrate on the ideas, the relationships, and developing personal meaning, while others put more effort into examining the logic of the argument and relating evidence to conclusions within the article itself. This difference seems to be attributable to contrasting styles of learning, which we shall come to later.

There are also differences between subject areas in the processes required to carry through the deep approach. Thus the emphasis on facts and internal logic will be correct for most scientific articles, while a greater concern with personal experience would be appropriate in the humanities.

It would also be wrong to give the impression that *students* can be categorised as 'deep' or 'surface'. Their approaches vary to some extent from task to task and from teacher to teacher. It is the *approach* which is categorised, *not* the student. Nevertheless, the relative balance between using deep or surface approaches does reflect differences between individuals and can be measured using an inventory (see Appendix).

Styles of learning

Gordon Pask[77] investigated the ways in which students tackled a task which required understanding. In one experiment the task involved working out the principles underlying a biological taxonomy – the differences between different sub-species of an imaginary animal – the Gandlemuller. From this and other experiments Pask distinguished two distinctive *styles of learning* – *holist* and *serialist* – which represent consistent preferences for using certain learning processes. A holist style involved a preference for setting the task in the broadest possible perspective and using visual imagery and personal experience to build up understanding. Illustrations, analogies, and anecdotes seem to be an essential part of holist learning. When asked to explain what has been learned, a holist explanation tends to be idiosyncratic and personalised. For example, one student gave this description of the Gandlemuller taxonomy:

> I want to tell you about a funny Martian animal which has been recently discovered and classified by scientists conducting surveys. They are funny sluglike things with various protuberances. These animals are called Gandlemullers, because they churn about in the swamps near the Equator and Gandle is the Martian for swampmud, hence the swampmudmuller (Müller is German for miller). These things churn through the mud eating it by some curious process which means they eat and excrete at the same time (page 91).[36]

After considerable elaboration, this student showed that all the principles of classification had been understood, but there was also redundant and even incorrect information. For example, the student had no information that the Gandlemuller had been 'recently discovered' or that it was 'friendly' (mentioned later in the student's description). These are examples of the information presented being reinterpreted from a personal standpoint. The *student* had 'recently discovered' the Gandlemuller, and drawings of the animals were interpreted as showing them to be 'friendly'.

In contrast, a serialist style is described by Pask as step-by-step learning. The focus is narrow, with the student concentrating on each step of the argument in order and in isolation. Facts and information are interpreted cautiously and critically, and little use is made of visual imagery or personal experience. Logic, rather than intuition, is the main intellectual instrument of understanding. Serialistic explanations tend to be carefully structured and clearly presented, but may be dull and humourless.

Explaining the Gandlemuller taxonomy, for example, a student who had relied on serialist learning said:

Zoologists have classified the Gandlemuller on the basis of physical characteristics. The three main types are Gandlers, Plongers, and Gandleplongers. Gandlers have no sprongs. Plongers have two sprongs. Gandleplongers have one sprong. There are four subspecies of Gandler: M1, M2, B1, and B2. The M's have one body, the B's have two bodies. The M1 and B1 have a single cranial mound. The M2 and B2 have a double cranial mound . . . etc. (page 91)[36]

It will be clear from these descriptions that holist styles are more suitable for learning in the humanities, and serialist styles in the sciences. But for many tasks, particularly in the sciences, elements of both styles are required. Pask found some students who were *versatile*: they were equally comfortable with either holist or serialist styles and used each as appropriate. Other students, however, showed marked over-reliance on one or other of the styles, and such students showed characteristic *pathologies of learning*. An unbalanced holist style led to a search for similarities between ideas without recognising important differences, using inappropriate analogies, generalising from inadequate evidence, and jumping to conclusions too readily. Pask called this *globetrotting*. Students using unbalanced serialist styles took no notice of important similarities, noting instead relatively trivial differences. They failed to use useful analogies and were reluctant to reach independent conclusions or make personal interpretations of evidence – a pathology of *improvidence*.

Not only did students with consistent imbalance in learning styles show pathologies which affected their general level of understanding, they also reacted differently to contrasting forms of instruction. Pask[43] produced programmed learning materials designed according to serialist and holist principles and then allocated students to these materials according to their learning styles. Students were matched and mismatched – holists with holist materials, holists with serialist materials, and serialists likewise. There was almost no overlap in the marks obtained after learning. The weakest of the matched students did almost as well as the best of the mismatched students. Whereas Skinner had argued that tightly organised material with step-by-step progression would be ideal for everyone, Pask demonstrated that this method of instruction was effective only for students who preferred a serialist style of learning. It was very ineffective for holists.

This finding immediately raises the question of whether teachers use holist and serialist teaching styles and, if so, what effects these may have – but this important issue will be discussed later. For the time being we shall concentrate on approaches and styles and ask how it is that each of these concepts has just two categories – deep/surface and holist/serialist.

The two distinct learning styles can be seen as the expression within the classroom of the contrasting cognitive styles described in the previous chapter. And so the existence of just two styles is explicable in terms of the main functions of the two cerebral hemispheres of the brain. Thus a holist style is equivalent to the cognitive style described as divergent, impulsive and global, while the serialist style involves convergent, reflective, and articulated processes. The holist style may thus depend on right hemisphere functions – visual, acoustic and kinaesthetic perceptions; passive, subsconscious, or incidental memorisation; and holistic or spatial reasoning. The serialist style similarly may draw on left hemisphere specialisations – linguistic, symbolic and semantic perceptions; conscious intentional memorising; and logical, sequential or analytic reasoning.

The two approaches to learning similarly can be seen as requiring the predominant use of different memory processes. The surface approach relies on rote-learning through repetition and rehearsal in short-term memory until a verbatim representation of the material is embedded in episodic long-term memory. The deep approach depends on meaningful learning utilising connections between concepts in semantic long-term memory. The meaning of the material is created through a web of inter-connections which will include episodic as well as semantic schemata if personal experience is utilised.

While it cannot be maintained that the link between styles or approaches and fundamental cerebral processes has been firmly established, the parallels are sufficiently strong to provide at least a provisional explanation of the existence of two strong dichotomies in students' learning processes.

Styles and Approaches in Classrooms

The utility of these ways of describing studying has been repeatedly demonstrated among students in higher education, but are they also useful in describing classroom learning? Pask's research was conducted with pupils as well as students, and his findings indicate that it is possible to distinguish holist and serialist styles among pupils, at least at the top end of secondary school. Other research on cognitive styles[59] shows that arts sixth-formers tend to be stronger on divergent thinking, while scientists have higher scores on convergent thinking. It is not clear, however, to what extent these preferences are accentuated by the experience of specialisation in the sixth-form. Again in the literature on cognitive styles[61] there is considerable difficulty throughout the primary years in deciding which differences between pupils are stylistic and which are developmental. Until a full repertoire of effective intellectual processes has been developed, preferences between them cannot be detected with any certainty.

On the other hand, differences in approaches to learning have been detected even during the earliest years of schooling. Ingrid Pramling[81] investigated the conceptions of learning held by Swedish children aged from three up to eight years. She identified a development trend in which the youngest children associated learning only with doing or with getting older. Initially even the idea of deliberate practice was not seen as an available strategy. Knowledge was not recognised in the abstract nor was it seen as something which the individual could actively seek: it was something adults had, and passed on to children. By age six an increasing proportion of children saw the need for their own active involvement in learning a skill, but very few, even by age eight, recognised the possibilities of controlling their thinking processes in a similar way:

Anna: 6.8
E: Do you always understand what's in the book?
S: No.
E: What should you do if you don't understand?
S: You can ask your mummy or daddy, but if you're grown up, then you have to think it out for yourself.[81]

Commenting on this study, Ference Marton[65] drew attention to the fact that even within this age group differing approaches to learning could be detected:

[Pramling] was able to show that as soon as we set up a school-like situation, the difference between a deep and surface approach . . . appears. She describes a situation where 5–6 year old children were taught about various [geometrical shapes], such as a triangle, circle, square and so on. Afterwards the teacher asked them about what they had learned. Some children focused only on trying to come up with the right answers to the questions, while others connected what they had learned with the real world, beyond the immediate (classroom) situation.[65]

A deep approach becomes available to a child once the notion of individual activity in understanding has been grasped. But even then pupils may not realise what understanding involves in a new situation, or may not believe that understanding is required by the teacher.

Hazel Francis[48] has argued that a failure to understand the *purpose* of reading prevents some children from beginning to read for themselves:

In my own research . . . I have come to realise that . . . lack of understanding, or misunderstanding, can affect both motivation and strategies . . . Although I have found children who thought that learning to read would take a long time, . . . there were others who thought the ability would come at some future date as an immediate enlightenment. In that case, they felt, why worry now? . . . I have [even] found children who did not realise that when their teachers were reading stories to them there was any connection with the book except through the pictures, or even perhaps though some sort of ritual action . . . [Such] variations amongst children show . . . them to be individuals starting school with understandings and intentions of their own . . . [And] I found [that] . . . those who understood something of the written word as a language form learned steadily, sometimes very quickly indeed, and with little or no forgetting, whilst those who lacked such understanding and were motivated only by the expectations that this was what happened in school or by the desire to please, learned much more slowly and forgot quite frequently (pages 15–18).[48]

Implicit in this description is the distinction between deep and surface approaches among pupils shortly after entering school. But these approaches have been identified explicitly among secondary school pupils. Ian Selmes, in a book in this series called *Improving Study Skills*,[90] reported the results of interviews he had carried out with 16 year olds before and after O levels. He found that the defining features of deep and surface approaches could be clearly seen from the pupils' comments. For example, in relation to dictated notes in history, a pupil commented that

. . . they give the information that I have to learn for the syllabus . . . in fairly short sentences, so I can pick up the information that I need to learn for the exam fairly easily (page 120).[89]

The surface approach was predominant at O level, being seen to be what was required by the examination questions. For the Scottish Highers at 17+ or A level at 18+, however, some pupils had realised the need to adopt a deep approach – at least in some tasks and some subjects:

In biology nothing is ever clear-cut so you've got to represent [in essays] two, three or perhaps four arguments and then try to say at the end which one seems most likely, but why it might not be . . .

[A history essay] gives you a chance to think for yourself, . . . to set down your interpretation, . . . so you can . . . compare your ideas with a good historian's.

What I do [in note-taking] is take down what is on the board and make extra notes on what comes up in class and then after class I will go and get the textbook out as well, and rewrite the notes, adding bits from the textbook (pages 121, 122, 124).[89]

To some extent these comments reflect the greater independence allowed in schools after O level, and the growing interest of the pupils in specialist subjects. But there is more to it than that. They do imply that the whole conception of what is required in school learning is changing from simply the reproduction of facts towards a recognition of the importance of personal meaning:

Well what you've got to do is work through everything until you're quite sure you can see exactly how things are arrived at. You can't just learn things . . . You've got to look at how you get there. That's how you come to understand it (page 121).[89]

The influence of the conception of learning, and contrasting approaches to learning, on the ways pupils tackle classroom tasks has been identified across a wide age range. But approaches to learning reflect primarily not developmental trends, but individual responses to interest in the content and anxiety about assessment requirements.

The Effects of Interest and Anxiety

One of Marton's colleagues at Gothenburg, Anders Fransson, carried out an interesting experiment into the effects of interest and anxiety on approaches to learning.[49] He chose an article about proposed changes in the assessment procedures in the Education Department. He then selected students to take part in the experiment – some were taking Education and could therefore be expected to find the article relevant and interesting, and others were taking Sociology but not Education. The students were asked to read the article and be ready to answer questions afterwards, but under contrasting experimental conditions. With one group the researcher tried to create a relaxed condition, while in the other he introduced an element of stress. With the second group a large tape recorder was placed in front of the students and it was explained that after they had written their answers to the questions, one of the group would be asked to dictate the answers into the tape recorder, and these answers would then be discussed by the group as a whole. It was predicted that interest would facilitate a deep approach, while anxiety would induce a surface approach. There was, however, no statistically significant difference between either Education and Sociology students or relaxed and stressful conditions. This surprising finding led Fransson to re-analyse the results. He had asked the students after the experiment whether they had found the article interesting and how anxious they had felt. He discovered that some of the Sociology students had found the article very interesting, and some students had found even the relaxed condition anxiety-provoking. So he compared the approaches of those students who reported different *perceptions* of interest and anxiety. *Then* the results were significant. It was not the experimental conditions themselves, but how these were experienced, that affected approaches to studying. Students who found the article interesting were more likely to have adopted a deep approach, while those who reported anxiety had tended to rely on a surface approach.

Similar findings have come from surveys which have investigated relationships between motivation and approaches to learning.[41,42] In Chapter 1 several different forms of motivation were described: Table 3.2 summarises the links which have been established so far. Intrinsic motivation (or interest in the subject matter) is always closely related to a deep approach. Fear of failure (or assessment anxiety) is consistently associated with a surface approach.

Thus motivation can be seen to influence not just the degree of effort put into school work, but also the types of effort, and so the particular processes of learning which are utilised. Thus if competition is over-emphasised, the increased emphasis on extrinsic rewards will increase effort, but towards reproductive learning. Improving interest and relevance, and so intrinsic motivation, again raises the level of effort, but also helps to direct the pupil towards personal involvement in learning.

Besides showing these links between deep or surface approaches and motivation, the surveys also identified another approach which is related to the competitive form of motivation called 'need for achievement' or hope for success. Again this approach involved a distinctive intention – to obtain the highest possible marks. This was thus described as a *strategic approach*.[82] The processes used depended on what the student believed would produce the best 'pay-off'. Deep and surface approaches were both used, but what was most distinctive about the strategic approach was the use of well-planned and carefully organised study methods. This approach depends on a systematic management of time and effort geared to the perceived demands of the assessment procedures. A summary of the defining characteristics of the strategic approach was shown in Table 3.1, while Table 3.2 shows the links between approaches and contrasting forms of motivation. Although extreme forms of the strategic approach are likely to merge into a surface approach through excessive concern with marks, a moderate level combined with a deep approach is likely to combine high levels of attainment with personal understanding.

The more recent attempts at developing pupils' study strategies, as we shall see in Chapter 4, have moved from a preoccupation with the component skills (for example, note-taking, speed reading) to a concern with developing the student's awareness of his or her own approaches to learning, and a recognition of the importance of extracting personal meaning wherever possible and matching strategies to the task requirements. In other words, study skills are introduced within a more general framework which emphasises deep strategic approaches.

Table 3.2 Motivation and approaches to learning

Motivation	Intention	Approach	Processes
Intrinsic	Understand	Deep	Relate to previous knowledge and experience
Fear of Failure	Complete task requirements	Surface	Memorise discrete items of information
Need for Achievement	Obtain highest possible marks	Strategic	Allocate time, effort and approaches, according to 'pay-off'

Educational Orientations and Attitudes

Motivation can be viewed as forces acting on the individual which explain subsequent behaviour. But that is too mechanistic a view. Most human actions are purposive: they are directed towards some goal. Our approaches to learning, our study strategies, depend on what we see education offering us. What do we hope to gain from it? To what uses do we intend to put it? Liz Taylor[98] has shown the importance of what she has called *educational orientations*. These describe distinctive sets of values, motives and attitudes relating to an educational course, which can be used to explain a student's subsequent behaviour. Students have very different reasons for continuing their education which can be understood in terms of contrasting dominant motives. Taylor distinguishes four main orientations – vocational, academic, personal, and social. Each of these could be intrinsic or extrinsic to the course of study, as shown in Table 3.3. Although some students had a predominant motive, most students showed combinations of these orientations. Also, as students began their course, it was as if they each had an implicit *study contract*. They had decided what they wanted to get out of the course and the university experience, and they judged their success in terms of this personal contract rather than the institution's formal judgements on academic progress. The contract was, of course, often 'renegotiated' later as a result of what happened on the course, but it had a strong continuing influence on a student's reported level of satisfaction.

The importance of this research is in the way it reinforces the idea that students have their own reasons for studying which powerfully influence their approaches and achievements. Thus a strong orientation towards personal development is likely to lead to deep approaches to learning, whereas an extrinsic vocational orientation will be associated with a predominantly surface approach.[54] If this idea is extended into classroom learning it still applies, though in a less articulated form. Each pupil develops, an *academic self-concept* – an image of himself or herself as learner which contains an implicit study contract. Pupils develop expectations of how much effort they will put into different school activities, how much they will enjoy them, and how well they will do in them. This self-concept develops and changes over the school years but is powerfully influenced by the family and by the peer group.

Table 3.3 Students' orientation to higher education (adapted from Gibbs *et al.* (1984) 'The world of the learner' in F. Marton, D. J. Hounsell and N. J. Entwistle (eds) *The Experience of Learning*, Scottish Academic Press).

Orientation	Interest	Aim	Concerns
Vocational	Extrinsic	Obtaining a qualification	Perceived worth of qualification
	Intrinsic	Being well trained	Relevance to future career
Academic	Extrinsic	Progression up educational ladder	Academic progress and performance
	Intrinsic	Pursuing subject for its own sake	Choosing stimulating courses or topics
Personal	Extrinsic	Compensation for past failures	Reassuring comments and pass marks
	Intrinsic	Broadening horizons	New insights and challenges
Social	Extrinsic	Having a good time	Facilities for sport and social activities

It is worth looking back at the diagram on page 22 which describes Béla Kozéki's theory of school motivation. The same influences apply to the self-concept, as Robert Burns argues:

Children arrive at school for the first time with a predisposition towards achievement or failure already engendered by the amount of parental interest, love and acceptance offered them. Each child has formed fairly firm pictures of his self worth which provides him with an array of self expectations about how he will behave in his school work and how others will react to him as a person. Each is already invisibly tagged, some enhancingly by a diet of nourishing interest and affections, and others crippled by a steady downpour of psychic blows from significant others denting, weakening, and distorting their self-concepts. So children enter the school milieu with a self-concept already forming, but still susceptible to modification. Teachers and peer groups begin to replace parents as a major source of information. With their aura of expertise, authority and evaluation, teachers are 'significant others' who feed the pupils' self-concepts with a menu of positive, neutral, and negative reinforcement, and create an ethos in the relationship which may enhance or debase academic performance . . . How many teachers have, without realising the implications, unleashed such barbs as:

'Ann, come to the front, as you are the smallest.'
'John, you never get it right, do you?'
'What a silly girl you are.'

Other children frequently receive such positive remarks as:

'Mary, take this message to the headmaster, I can trust you to remember it.'
'Good boy, look at what Peter has done everybody.'
'Frank, you're a strong boy, come and help me move this desk.'

The normal run-of-the-mill verbalisations of the teacher are fraught with evaluation and expectations of pupils. But few teachers have realised how potent it all is (pages 276, 288).[22]

Burns sees a circular process of developing and reinforcing children's self-concepts. The initial levels of performance create expectations which are then communicated by the teachers and confirm the developing ideas of self worth. Where the initial performance is poor, this circle can become a vicious circle of demoralisation.

Recent research has investigated the reasons pupils give for their success or failure in school – in technical terms their causal attributions. Internal attributions describe success or failure in terms of the pupil's own effort or ability. External attributions explain the outcome in terms of the difficulty or easiness of the task, or as a matter of luck. Martin Covington[27] is concerned about the problems low ability children have in accounting for their poor performance. He argues that it is damaging to the self-image for such children to admit to having low ability, so they are likely to attribute failure to external factors – the teacher's prejudice, unreasonably difficult lessons, or continuing bad luck. But another acceptable explanation is lack of effort. The danger in attributing poor performance to lack of effort is that pupils come to believe that explanation, and they then opt out of trying. With low ability, effort is of crucial importance in building up levels of performance which would also create more self-confidence. Yet if they do try hard, and still are found lacking, the feeling of humiliation can be even stronger, as Martin Covington points out:

> The realities of classroom life make untenable such crude and obvious tactics as simply not trying. Teachers value effort; they reward success more and punish failure less when the student has tried hard . . . Thus many students must thread their way between the threatening extremes of high effort and no effort at all. It is for this reason that effort has been characterised as a 'double-edged sword'. Excuses chiefly in the form of rationalisations or other forms of denial are the student's basic ally in achieving this precarious balance. Attributionally, excuses function to externalise blame for failure away from the internal, stable element of ability . . . Excuses . . . maintain a balance between trying and not trying, . . . [and] reduce student shame and feelings of worthlessness regardless of effort level . . . We can [thus] piece together the elements of a safe strategy for students when risking failure, designed to minimise teacher punishment and reduce, at least temporarily, the shame and humiliation that accompanies failure. Try, or at least, appear to try, but not too energetically and with excuses always handy! (pages 147, 149)[27]

While experiences in school markedly affect the academic self-concept, parents and peers have a strong and continuing influence. The attitudes of parents and peers are often taken to reflect the social class or ethnic origins of the group to which the pupil belongs. It is certainly true that different social classes or ethnic minorities, as groups, will hold identifiable sets of attitudes and values. But the teacher deals not with groups but with individuals. And within each group the variations in attitudes or self-concept are too large to make sensible predictions on the basis of group membership alone. As Burns comments:

> Low social class membership cannot be a sufficient cause of academic failure since not all pupils from the low social class perform poorly at school. Similarly, not all middle-class children achieve high levels of academic attainment . . . If the self-concept is below a threshold point then not even middle-class children of high ability will do well (page 282).[22]

Nevertheless, the strength of peer group influences are such that in some inner-city schools attitudes to education and academic self-concepts will be generally negative, thus making it difficult for pupils to express their individuality. And the failure of many parents to take sufficient responsibility for the behaviour and attitudes of their children can become an insuperable handicap to teachers. Yet, where parents have been encouraged to provide systematic help under school guidance, considerable improvements in attainment have been reported.[100]

Among adolescent girls, the peer group begins increasingly to emphasise personal appearance and social relationships at the expense of academic attainments. Also sex stereotyping becomes a powerful influence on choice of subjects. The way some girls suddenly reject mathematics and the physical sciences is both striking and puzzling.[2] Margaret Sutherland[97] suggests that 'competition by the opposite sex in the classroom changes pupils' estimates of their own strengths and weaknesses'. She goes on to describe research which found that teachers made different types of comment to boys and girls:

> Since teachers' comments often relate to boys' behaviour or lack of attention rather than to errors in their work, boys' confidence in their ability to cope with a subject may remain strong, but since girls are expected to have worked hard, comment to them is more likely to point out errors in their work, so feedback may give them the impression of insufficient ability (page 178).[97]

Sutherland comments, in line with Covington's views, that such differential interpretations may be particularly damaging to self-confidence as boys are being charged with lack of effort, which can be changed, while girls are being accused of lack of ability, which is seen by pupils as irredeemable.

There may, of course, still be teachers reinforcing the sex stereotype of girls being unable to cope with rigorous scientific thinking or of boys lacking mature aesthetic or emotional responses. The continuing public denunciation of such attitudes should, however, be reducing, if not eliminating, its occurrence in the classroom.

What we are left with is emphatic evidence of the importance of a pupil's self-concept in affecting the approach to learning and influencing the more general orientation towards education. Ways of helping pupils to develop positive, yet realistic, self-concepts will be discussed towards the end of the book. Now we turn to the implications of the various theories for classroom learning.

Summary

Investigations of learning from the pupil's perspective draw attention to the importance of *intention* in learning. A *deep approach* involves the intention to understand, and attempts to relate incoming information to previous knowledge and experience in order to extract personal meaning. In a *surface* approach, the intention is to fulfil the task requirements, which leads to memorisation of only what is thought to be required by the teacher. A *strategic approach* also focuses on the assessment requirements, but with the intention to obtain the highest possible marks by a systematic allocation of time and effort.

Students seeking understanding may still use distinctive processes. A *holist style* represents a preference for a broad perspective, drawing on a wide variety of analogies and illustrations in building up a personalised form of understanding. A *serialist style* involves step-by-step learning with a narrow focus on evidence, cautious interpretation and logical analysis.

The approach to learning is influenced by the student's perception of the task and its setting. *Interest* or intrinsic motivation facilitates a deep approach, while *anxiety* or fear of failure induces a surface approach. A *need for achievement* is associated with the strategic approach.

Students differ in their *orientations* to education and have implicit study contracts against which they judge their success. In schools these contracts become part of an *academic self-concept* which is strongly influence by family and peer group and which in turn influences classroom behaviour and learning. Teachers have a particularly potent influence on the academic self-concept through the comments they make about the pupils' competence and efforts.

Social class, sex, or ethnic origin, in themselves, may be misleading indicators of the attitudes or academic self-concepts of an individual pupil, but there is no doubt that attitudes are powerfully affected by the peer group. Stereotyping, of whatever sort, is potentially damaging to the development and academic progress of the pupil.

4

Managing Classroom Learning

In the previous chapter different learning approaches and outcomes were explained mainly in terms of other characteristics of the learner. Deep approaches depended on interest; surface approaches and low attainment were attributed to anxiety and poor self-concept. But it was not intended to suggest that the pupil has the sole responsibility for these approaches and outcomes. It was indicated that motivation and attitudes are affected by parents and teachers. In this chapter, learning is examined within the classroom context. In what ways do *teachers* influence learning? How can some of the ideas derived from theories of learning be applied in practice? Already the earlier chapters have included indications of certain classroom implications, but here some of the more recent classroom research is discussed. Teachers are responsible for managing classroom learning. What principles should they keep in mind?

In Chapter 1 a framework was introduced to serve as one organising principle for the book. It showed how learning theories varied in terms of the extent to which control of learning was given to the teacher or the pupil. This is a crucial issue in considering learning in the classroom context. Attempts at providing detailed suggestions for classroom management derive from learning theories and retain the assumptions about control implicit in their origins. Thus we shall see the influence of behaviourism, information processing, constructivist and experiential learning theories in the following sections.

The starting point is the continuing influence of stimulus-response theories and the techniques of programmed learning, through computer-based learning and mastery learning. Strong teacher control is involved in these procedures and is implied in recent research on task analysis derived from information processing theory, and in some of the work on time and task management. But even within this research the emphasis is shifting to take account of pupils' perceptions of teachers' requirements. The constructivist, the aptitude, stage or task matching, and the experiential theories of learning all bring with them a recognition of the complex interactions between the learner and the classroom context, which form the basis of the later sections, and of the final chapter.

Computer-based Learning

One of the limitations in the development of programmed learning was that the more sophisticated branching programmes were difficult to present effectively. The format of the book, or even of the teaching machine, made routing through different frames slow and cumbersome. The advent initially of mainframe computers, and more recently of microcomputers, has provided a machine for presenting sophisticated programmed instruction. It has been suggested that computer-based learning 'stands or falls on the merits of programmed learning, for the computer is simply the means of increasing its convenience to the pupil.' This view of computer-based learning is the popular image supported by a wide range of educational software, and yet Tim O'Shea and John Self,[75] in one of the most recent books on this topic, dismiss that view as 'complete nonsense'. It is true that early examples of computer-based learning were modelled almost exclusively on programmed learning, but more recent work draws on ideas from information processing and artificial intelligence.

Many cognitive psychologists have used computers to test out theories about the ways in which humans store and process information, and their theories have then been used to develop techniques by which computers can parallel human problem-solving activities. This attempt to program computers to mimic human thought processes has led to a new research area called 'artificial intelligence' which, in turn, is suggesting ways in which computers could go beyond presenting just frames of information, but could also respond 'intelligently' to the difficulties being experienced by the individual pupil. Computers are already being programmed to act as 'expert systems' which use stored information to make deductions. For example, an illness might be diagnosed for a doctor by a computer which contains not just the most recent evidence on symptoms, but also the equivalent of the diagnostic procedures used by the top specialists in that illness. The computer has both information and a set of rules to interpret particular patterns of data.

Already computers have been used in classrooms as data bases which pupils search to identify information relevant to, for example, project work. And computers allied to video discs are able to store not only text, diagrams and photographs, but also video or film material. They can thus provide either a versatile medium for pupil exploration or sophisticated visual aids for the teacher.

Besides being able to store, identify and process information, computers are, of course, capable of carrying out complex calculations in fractions of a second. It is this facility that has been used to create simulations of complex processes. If the process can be translated into a series of mathematical formulae, then pupils can investigate for themselves the effects of varying the parameters involved. For example, the level of pollution of a pond depends on time, on the animal and the plant life, and on the types and concentrations of pollutants. By varying these contributory factors systematically pupils can visualise the reality behind the principles built into the underlying model. Computers are also being used to simulate lengthy or dangerous scientific experiments, and to control scientific apparatus.

Word processing is widely used in commercial organisations and in business studies courses in school and colleges. But computer programs could also be used to help pupils produce more effective written work by guiding both their initial planning and allowing opportunities for easy editing or reorganising. Already the severe communication difficulties of pupils with physical handicaps have been ameliorated through the use of microcomputers.[73] Moreover, pupils who show little interest in school work have been motivated by the use of programs which use games to encourage the development of, for example, basic arithmetical skills, while the microcomputer can provide inexhaustible patience and encouragement in allowing slow learners the opportunity of practising repeatedly.

Finally, the skills of computer programming itself have been used to encourage logical thinking and problem-solving. Some computer languages, such as LOGO, are particularly well suited for this purpose. Seymour Papert[76] has argued that more sophisticated developments in computer programming will soon provide learning environments with a 'high potential for personal involvement, intellectual adventure and cognitive enhancement'.

While there is already little doubt that the advent of microcomputers has provided opportunities for learning which go well beyond the simple extension of programmed learning, we still know very little either about the types of learning stimulated by the different modes of program (games, simulations, drill and practice) or about the extent to which intellectual skills learned with computers are transferable to other situations.[57,75] Without substantial research into the effects of working with computers, it is very difficult to be sure which techniques will provide teachers with important *new* ways of facilitating the types of learning they want to encourage.

The term computer-based learning has been coined to cover both computer-aided instruction (CAI) and computer-managed learning. The various programming modes described above are mainly examples of CAI. In computer-managed learning the role of the computer is quite different. It may be used to guide pupils through a set of printed resource materials or work-cards. The computer may present and score tests on the pupil's prior learning, and on the basis of that score allocate the next piece of work. The computer might also not only keep a cumulative record of test scores, but also diagnose specific difficulties to draw to the attention of both pupil and teacher.[68] This offers a form of classroom management previously not available to the teacher.

Computers have also been used to store item banks. These contain questions initially written by teachers, but subsequently carefully tested and classified in terms of both topic area and level of difficulty. From each bank teachers can obtain tests pre-selected by the computer to be tailor-made for their own class, but based on national norms. Again diagnosis of recurring errors could be carried out by computer, although more work on the nature of the errors would be needed first. An extension of the techniques of item banking would utilise video discs to allow resource material to be classified and stored in a similar way to items.[74]

With this wide range of possible uses, it may be wondered why microcomputers have not made a greater impact on education. One of the main reasons is that the generation of microcomputers introduced initially into schools had very limited storage and power. The next generation of machines should provide more realistic opportunities, but again it would require a massive national investment in software development and extensive in-service training programmes to realise the potential of microcomputers in education. It would require a major policy change, however, to allow such investment: without it the innovative possibilities of computers will be lost to education.

Mastery Learning

James Block describes mastery learning as

> . . . an optimistic theory about teaching and learning . . . (which asserts) that virtually all students can master a great deal of what they are taught in school if the instruction is approached systematically, if students are helped when and where they are having learning difficulties, if they are given sufficient time to achieve mastery, and if there is some clear criterion of what constitutes mastery (page 6;[11] page 265[12]).

'Mastery' implies that pupils will obtain nearly full marks, because they will be tested only when they decide they are ready.

The impetus for mastery learning again originates in programmed learning, but takes more account of individual differences and recognises the crucial influence of 'time'. The course material is broken down into logically ordered elements with feedback after each element. Students who do not reach the prescribed standard go over the content again. And at the end of the course there is an objective test to indicate the overall level of attainment. The crucial difference from programmed learning is that mastery learning breaks the content down not into frames but into 'blocks' which may be large enough to represent the more familiar topics identifiable by teachers. The technique also takes account of the need to encourage motivation and provides ways of managing mixed-ability classes to allow for differences in the speed with which pupils learn.

Benjamin Bloom[14] who wrote one of the most influential texts explaining the principles of mastery learning, drew attention to the correspondence between the distribution of scores in 'intelligence' tests and attainment tests. If a large number of pupils are given, for example, a verbal reasoning test, the distribution of scores will generally follow what is called a 'normal curve' – the familiar bell-shaped curve in which the majority of scores are around the average with progressively fewer scores found towards either extreme. When teachers give an end of term test to a whole year group, the scores again typically follow the normal curve with only few pupils obtaining very high marks. Bloom attacked the ready acceptance of this distribution of marks, regarding it as a failure in teaching. If instead of regarding intelligence as limiting the ability to learn, it is seen as affecting the speed with which people learn, then the attainment curve could be pushed up towards the high end by organising teaching in ways which allow the slower pupils more time and more encouragement.

In its idealised form, mastery learning is individualised to allow each pupil to progress at his or her own rate. This involves the teacher in preparing a great deal of carefully graded resource material, and is also difficult to fit into the normal school pattern of teaching. However, James Block[12] had described how the principles of mastery learning may be adapted to the normal demands of a school curriculum.

The objectives of the course are carefully defined and a final examination paper is prepared to test the attainment of each of these objectives. Next, the level of mastery required is decided, usually fixed at about 80% of full marks. The course is then divided up into units and these are organised into the most appropriate order. There are four components associated with each unit: the main teaching material, a diagnostic test on the content of the unit, a set of remedial materials, and enrichment materials.

At the beginning of the course the teacher explains both the objectives and the principles of mastery learning. It is emphasised that all the pupils should be able to master most of the main units. At the beginning of each new unit the pupils are encouraged to think about what they have already achieved as a way of fostering competence motivation (against the pupil's own standards) rather than competitive motivation (against other pupils' standards). The initial teaching within mastery learning will follow the normal teaching pattern of exposition, class discussion where appropriate, and written work. At the end of each unit, however, the diagnostic test is given. Pupils who reach the defined level of mastery are allocated to the enrichment material which allows them to explore themes related to the unit, and they may also be asked to act as peer-tutors, helping other pupils. Those who fail to demonstrate mastery are allocated to remedial materials which take them over the content of the unit again, but in a different way. These pupils begin by discussing their diagnostic test results with the teacher to discover their main weaknesses or misunderstandings. This procedure allows their effort to be focused in the most productive ways to ensure that mastery is achieved at the next test.

Inevitably mastery learning over the first few units of a course takes much longer than conventional approaches. But it does seem that the thorough learning of the initial units allows later units to be completed more quickly. Thus a mastery learning course can be completed within normal time allocations. Although not all pupils will reach mastery in the time available, evaluations[13] suggest that achievement levels are raised overall, the proportion of low marks in the end of unit examination is substantially reduced, and pupils show positive attitudes to the content of mastery learning courses and to the opportunities for co-operative learning. Although mastery learning has not been adopted in its original form to any large extent outside North America, the idea of core content associated with extensions or repetition has become the basis of many effective approaches to mixed-ability teaching.

Time and Task Management

Mastery learning has been used predominantly in secondary education, but some of its principles have been incorporated into a model of teaching and learning for primary schools developed by Neville Bennett.[5] This model is also based on systematic observation of the behaviour of teachers and pupils in classrooms.[7,8,51] His main idea is that the task of the teacher is to manage 'the attention and time of

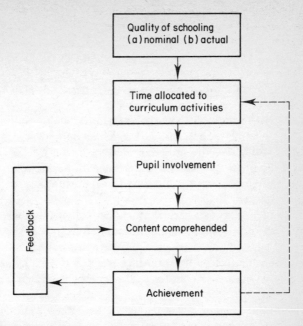

Figure 4.1 A model of teaching-learning processes (from S. N. Bennett (1985) 'Time and teach: teaching-learning processes in primary school' in N. J. Entwistle (ed.) *New Directions in Educational Psychology – Learning and Teaching*, Falmer Press)

pupils in relation to the educational ends of the classroom'.[5] The model itself is shown in Figure 4.1.

Within this model, learning depends above all on the length of time allocated to different curriculum areas and on the quality of the pupils' involvement with the learning activities allocated to them. In Britain, local authorities, schools, and teachers determine the content and balance of the primary curriculum with advice from school inspectors and government circulars. The result of this independence is a considerable variation in the time spent on different curriculum areas. Bennett summarises the results of several surveys which, taken together, indicate that while

. . . the average time spent on say mathematics (five hours) and language (seven hours) are consistent, variations between teachers are large. For example, in mathematics some teachers stated that they spend less than one hour per week whereas others devote eight hours to this subject . . . Some teachers felt that [it] . . . should be taught daily, others four days per week, whilst a minority group felt that no regular commitment was necessary . . . (page 257).[5]

These variations are particularly worrying when viewed in conjunction with the fact that, on the whole, attainment levels were found to be related to the time allocated to the subject. Thus the policy of the school and the individual teacher in deciding curriculum priorities will control the pupils' opportunities to make academic progress.

However, it is not just curriculum allocation which affects pupil learning. Teachers differ widely in the extent to which they are able to maintain pupil involvement in learning. In primary schools there are various activities going on which relate to administration, transitions between tasks, and social interactions, rather than to learning itself.

When Bennett[7] made observations of the percentage of time spent 'on task' in open-plan classrooms he found an average of 61% for the 5–7 year olds and 66% for the 7–11 year olds. But again variations between teachers were large – from 50% up to 80%. Moreover, when the time spent on task by individual pupils was examined, an even larger variation was found – from 20% to nearly 90%.

Some aspects of classroom management seem to affect time spent on task. For example, Kevin Wheldall has reported the effects on behaviour produced by changing from group work to individual work at desks.[103] On-task behaviour increased from 70% for group work to 86% for individual work and back to 71% when returning to groups. Bennett[6] draws attention to similar findings which suggest that, besides a lower time spent on task, even when pupils do discuss their work in groups, the interactions are unlikely to foster effective learning. Observations indicated that

. . . the great majority of requests and responses were of a low order – a specific question, for example, 'How many two's in fifty-four?', followed by a specific response, and not all responses were correct. Explanations were rare (page 115).[6]

These findings should not be taken to justify a wholesale reversion to individual desk work, but rather that conditions have to be created within the classroom to allow pupils adequate time for concentrated work 'on task', as well as providing opportunities to develop collaborative and social skills.

The actual time spent on task is a necessary but not sufficient condition for learning. Observation studies cannot determine the way in which pupils spend their time on task – the *quality* of their involvement. Teachers can influence the quality of attention through what Bennett describes as levels of 'comprehension'. He argues that many pupils fail to learn effectively because of poor 'matching'. The tasks they are given are inappropriate to their ability level. This problem is particularly severe among the top and bottom thirds of the ability range. He suggests that the most effective teachers make more substantial demands on their pupils than other teachers, but those demands are well matched to pupils' abilities.

Bennett's review of the research evidence leads him to the conclusion that:

> The lower ability pupils learn more by having less taught to them, and by having it taught redundantly to the point of overlearning (i.e. repetitively), proceeding in small steps that they can master without undue cognitive strain. In contrast, higher ability children can cover the same material more quickly and furthermore will learn optimally by being challenged with . . . more difficult questions and assignments' (page 260).[5]

Task Analysis

The behaviouristic origins of Bennett's model are clear, even though teacher control is being exercised in a realistic classroom setting. There is still room only for major differences in intellectual ability, in deciding teaching strategies. The active role of the learner, and the differing perceptions of classroom tasks, are left out of his analysis.

Another recent development in research on classroom learning, in which Bennett has also been involved,[8] has included the detailed analysis of the processes by which pupils tackle everyday classroom tasks. These studies began from an information-processing perspective, examining pupils' procedures in relation to common errors – the so-called 'buggy algorithms' or faulty procedures. More recently, however, the research has introduced a 'constructivist' perspective, with the pupil being seen as active in constructing meaning from the task itself, and in interpreting the teacher's requirements.

In the USA, Lauren Resnick[84] has been reporting a wide range of such studies, particularly relating to elementary mathematics. How do children carry out addition and subtraction? The textbooks show how it should be done, but children seem to develop intuitive rules of their own. Many of these rules are nearly correct, but importantly wrong. They produce right answers for a proportion of questions and leave teachers puzzling where the errors have come from. On the other hand, some of the intuitive methods are more elegant than the formal methods generally taught. Resnick explains what happens in single-digit addition and subtraction.

Textbooks typically teach addition as a process of counting out the two named subsets and then recounting the combined set, and everyone expects children rather quickly to give up any kind of counting in favour of memorising the addition 'facts'. However, experiments have now revealed that there is an intermediate period during which children continue to solve problems by counting – but not by the method initially taught in school. Instead, they use a procedure that seems to imply an understanding of commutivity and that is elegantly simpler than the procedure taught. This procedure, typical of 6 year olds and up, is known as the *min* model, because the smaller (minimum) of the two addends is added to the other in a counting-on procedure. For example, to add 3 + 5, the child starts at 5 (even though it is named second) and counts on '5 . . . 6, 7, 8'. . . A similar story can be told for subtraction . . . [children] *either* count down from the minuend *or* count up from the subtrahend, *whichever will take the fewest counts*. Thus for 9 − 2 they say '9 . . . 8, 7', but for 9 − 7, they say '7 . . . 8, 9' . . . Children who invent these procedures behave as if they understand the commutivity principle of addition, and the complementarity of addition and subtraction. However, it is not yet clear how explicit such understanding actually is (page 21).[84]

Many of the errors children make in simple arithmetic prove not to be random slips, but the application of faulty intuitive rules. They are often quite sensible approaches, wrong only in perhaps one aspect. Once these faulty procedures have been catalogued, it should be possible to help teachers to spot them, and also devise computer programs which will detect at least some of them from pupils' interactions with the computer. One recurring problem seems to be a failure to understand the procedure of 'borrowing'. Resnick has investigated the use of a technique to help pupils see the parallel between concrete representations of borrowing and the numerical formalism. Work cards show the problem, for example, 300 − 129. The pupil draws three large blocks and writes the numbers one under the other, in the normal way, alongside. The bottom block of 'hundreds' is then split up into 10 smaller blocks of 'tens' and the notation of borrowing is again written alongside. A similar step is applied to 'tens' and 'units'. The technique of making subtraction concrete is, of course, well-known. What is new is a realisation that some children fail to make the connection between their concrete experiences and the abstract notations. That insight can be provoked by emphasising the parallelism in a direct way.

Although such research is still at its early stages, it does show the importance of providing learning materials which help pupils through 'natural' stages in developing understanding. It is too easy for adults to teach a 'right' way, which is too formal or too abstract for children to follow. Or for them to assume that analogies between concrete and abstract representations will easily be followed by children. As Resnick comments:

In traditional instructional design it was tacitly assumed that a task analysis that specified the performance or knowledge of skilled people in a domain would automatically yield not only 'objectives' for instruction, but an outline of the form in which information should be presented to learners. Implicit in this assumption was the notion that instruction should communicate as directly as possible the 'mature' or 'expert's' form of knowledge. [Recent] research . . . makes it clear that this assumption does not adequately recognise the work of the learner in *constructing* the mature form of knowledge . . . [It seems] then the task of the instructor is not to search for ways of presenting information that directly match the thought or performance patterns of experts. Rather, it is to find instructional representations that allow learners to gradually construct these expert representations for themselves (page 31).[84]

Charles Desforges[31] and his colleagues have been widening the analysis of classroom tasks to take account of the context more directly. The currency of the classroom is the teacher's marks and comments: the pupils try 'to deliver what the teacher is predicted to reward'. In trying to please the teacher, pupils go to great lengths to disguise their misunderstandings – a procedure which, of course, prevents the teacher from giving effective help with the difficulties. Pupils have to take account not just of the academic content of the task and the teacher's direct instructions, but also the 'hidden curriculum' – what it is that really gets rewarded. The rewards do not always tally with the instructions, as Charles Desforges discovered:

A teacher was recently observed to talk to a class of 6 year old children . . . about the countries of origin of the produce commonly found in fruit shops . . . She finished by asking the children to 'write me an exciting story about the fruit we eat'. The children had to decide what she meant by this! They were helped in part by the fact that they had heard the instruction before in respect of other contents. In fact the children wrote very little. They took great pains to copy the date from the board. (The teacher did not ask them to do this. It was presumably taken for granted as part of the task specification.) They formed their letters with great care and used rubbers copiously to correct any slips of presentation. Whilst this went on the teacher moved about the class commending 'neat work' and 'tidy work' and chiding children for 'dirty fingers' and 'messy work'. No further mention was made of 'exciting' content or of 'stories'. It seemed that the children knew perfectly well what the teacher meant when she asked for an 'exciting story about fruit' even though in this case the overt task definition (the teacher's instructions) stood in sharp contrast . . . to the reward structure (pages 168–9).[32]

Desforges argues that it is important for the teacher to reward with marks and comments the main objectives of the teaching.

Unless the reward structure reinforces the required behaviour, pupils will continue to spend time on inappropriate activities. Even major changes in curriculum or the updating of teachers' subject knowledge may have little effect, if teaching patterns and reward structures remain as they are:

> [Yet] apparently minor alterations to teaching behaviour might be expected to demand major readaptations on the part of pupils. For example, if a teacher adopted a policy of occasional but detailed interviews with each child in which the child's capacity to reveal his thinking processes was rewarded (as opposed to his capacity to fill a page neatly), children might be expected to develop ways of meeting this new demand. It would not be possible, or necessary, to interview all children on all tasks: it would be sufficient that the child expected to get such an inter-view – and that occasionally he did. Such an apparently minor change requires great skill and planning in its execution and interpretation. Done clumsily, the interview turns into an inter-rogation focusing on the child's weaknesses. Children might then adapt by staying away from school. But interviews based on developing specific competencies could help the teacher better to understand the pupil's difficulties and the child to learn that schooling rewards the development of personal understanding and not simply the reproduction of 'correct answers' (page 170).[32]

In this final phrase Desforges is describing the main defining features of deep and surface approaches, and suggesting how the teacher should use rewards to encourage a deep approach. But this is just one of the ways in which approaches are influenced by context.

Facilitating Deep Approaches

In classrooms, the tasks presented to pupils are almost always set in an assessment context. The approach to learning adopted by the pupil involves differing focuses of attention. In Chapter 2 the idea of a focus of attention was used to describe how concentration shifted from one sense to another. It is as if there is a tension between them. Intense concentration on, for example, listening, pulls the attention away from watching or touching. A similar tension can be seen between the three approaches to learning – deep, surface, and strategic – with attention being focused on personal meaning, satisfying the teacher, or competing with other pupils.

In the deep approach, attention is initially focused on meaning, but attempts to relate incoming information to previous knowledge and experience activate memories which can become distracting, even though they also provide potentially useful connections. In the surface approach, the student is distracted by the awareness of task requirements, worrying so much about what questions might be asked that the content itself moves into the background. The student adopting a strategic approach is also aware of task require-ments and assessment procedures, but sees these as opportunities to obtain high marks or to make a good impression. In spite of this more positive attitude, the attention paid to allocating time, effort, and resources efficiently can also deflect attention from what is being learned.

It is important to recognise that the way attention moves between the content and various peripheral aspects of the task is to some extent under the control of the teacher. Diana Laurillard,[63] investi-gated students' approaches to a problem which involved writing a device control program for a microprocessor. The students commented on how they set about the task:

> I read through the question to see what was familiar *from the lecture*, i.e. phrases or specific words that were repeated.

> I have to sort through the wording very slowly to understand *what he wants us to do*.

> I read through with *reference to the class notes* making sure I understand the sequence (page 130, italics added).[63]

Laurillard comments:

> We might expect that the first stages of solving such a problem would be to consider what kind of microprocessor it is, what kinds of control would be needed, which instructions are relevant, etc. But the students' attention is focused not on the program to be written, but rather on what they think the teacher requires . . . Each student, in different ways, relates the problem to its educa-tional context: the lecture, the lecturer, the lecture notes . . . The students (can) be so concerned to solve the problem *in its*

educational context that they pay little attention to the problem itself or its inherent subject matter content . . . So the problem-solving task may fail to ensure that the students learn about the subject matter. They do learn something about the 'problem-in-context', but that includes knowing about how to get good coursework marks, about reading between the lines, about interpreting a lecturer's behaviour, and so on (page 131–2).[63]

It is thus important for teachers to recognise how pupils' perceptions of a task may differ from their own. Teachers may see the task and the assessment as entirely separate. Pupils will almost certainly see the assessment as part of the task, and this different perception will affect their focus of attention.

In other studies the effects of differing types of assessment have been demonstrated. At university, students have commented on how the form of assessment affects their learning strategies. One student, for example, whose course involved regular short-answer questions, commented:

I hate to say it, but what you've got to do is to have a list of the 'facts'. You write down ten important points and memorise those, then you'll do all right in the test . . . If you can give a bit of factual information – so and so did that, and concluded that – for two sides of writing, then you'll get a good mark (page 144).[83]

An emphasis on factual questions seems to cause students, almost immediately, to adopt a surface approach. Multiple choice questions may be particularly strong in this effect unless they have been carefully designed to test understanding. In Britain, the tendency for 16 year olds to adopt surface approaches has been attributed to the nature of the external examinations, as Hungarian pupils of the same age predominantly utilise deep approaches.[41]

The choice of a particular mode of assessment reflects, in part, the characteristics of the subjects, but it also reflects the teacher's or the examiner's conception of what learning involves. As a result of their studies on qualitative differences in learning, Ference Marton and his colleagues[66] argued that their findings

[presented] in stark contrast, the taken-for-granted conception of learning as the accurate reproduction of a body of knowledge largely defined by the teacher, and a view of learning as a change in the learner's understanding, brought about by a reconstruction of ideas . . . [Following] the traditional view of knowledge . . . the teacher . . . will tend to ask essentially closed questions, expecting students to reproduce the facts or ideas previously presented. The student will be anxiously concerned about how to remember the information which, correctly reproduced, will complete the next step in the perceived course requirements. The alternative conception implies the asking of open questions, and the recognition that the answers will have interesting and revealing qualitative, even idiosyncratic, differences. The students are then encouraged to see learning as a reorganisation and transformation of their understanding of aspects of the real world (page 237).

In surveys of students, a clear relationship was established linking 'freedom in learning' and 'good teaching' with deep approaches. In departments where students felt they were given opportunities to choose what and how they learned, a higher proportion of them adopted a deep approach. 'Good teaching' in lectures was described in terms of 'level', 'pace', 'structure' and 'rapport'. But above all, in interviews, students stressed how striking explanations and enthusiasm affected their learning. For example, a physics student recounted how:

Recently we were doing Fourier analysis, and the lecturer mentioned in passing that it was something which they used when they transmit moon pictures back to earth . . . Another example he quoted was about how when you bang a drum you get lots of different sounds rather than when you, say, play a violin you just get one note . . . he said, if you look at this you can see why – and he was right, you could see why; it did make sense (page 145).[83]

Striking illustrations seem to help students both to share the teacher's enthusiasm vicariously and, in some instances, to shift both conceptions and approaches to learning. A detailed study of students' experiences of lectures led Vivien Hodgson[58] to conclude:

Vicarious experience of relevance can . . . be viewed as providing a bridge between extrinsic experience or a surface approach and intrinsic experience or a deep approach . . . to go beyond the outward demands of a learning situation and make connections between the content of the lecture and their understanding of the world around them (page 102).

Teachers thus play a crucial role, not just in transmitting information efficiently, but also in transforming ways of learning which would otherwise prevent personal understanding being attempted, let alone being achieved.

What students perceive as 'good teaching' will, of course, depend on their own conceptions of learning. Students who are intent on seeking understanding will appreciate lecturers who emphasise personal meaning. But students who have a reproductive conception of learning are more likely to emphasise the importance of efficient transfer of knowledge in simple language, without major intellectual demands.

In the secondary school, Ian Selmes[90] has reported similar links between teaching and approaches to learning. Pupils report adopting surface approaches in classes taught by methods which foster dependency – the transfer of condensed information from board or hand-out into the pupil's head. He also drew attention to the combined effects of a heavy workload and lack of time. A deep approach takes time; if too much is required too quickly, the pupils are forced to adopt surface strategies as a coping ploy. Discussions, or lively questioning by a teacher, arouse interest, reflection, and so a deep approach.

Other ways of encouraging a deep approach involve helping pupils to become more aware of their own learning strategies. Traditional study skills courses emphasise the development of individual *skills* such as note-taking or speed reading. These courses have not proved successful. John Nisbet and Janet Shucksmith[70] suggest that it is essential to show pupils how to use these skills in their everyday learning. They have to use a *strategy* – a set of procedures designed to achieve a certain purpose. An analogy is taken from football to explain this distinction. Ball control, dribbling, passing, are all component skills necessary to the footballer. But unless the player can use these appropriately at the right time he could not be called skilful. Moreover, the really good player looks ahead, reads the game, to change the pattern of play in a way which creates goal-scoring opportunities. Moving back to the classroom, the component skills are taught within school subjects, and strategies are often suggested for passing examinations. But what is lacking is the attempt to help pupils develop effective, general strategies for learning. Beyond skills and strategies, Nisbet and Shucksmith associate the deep *approach* to learning with the ability to think metacognitively about learning, reflecting on purpose and outcome. A deep approach can be seen as 'reading' the learning game, not just in terms of examination results, but also as a way of facilitating personal understanding. There has thus been a move away from teaching skills to emphasising the need for effective strategies and a deep approach to learning.

One way of encouraging this reflective approach to studying is to provide 'learning to learn' workshops which utilise the concept of 'deep approach'. The work of Ian Selmes[90] described in Chapter 3 led to the development of a course adapted from a conventional study skills course which helped sixth-formers not just to develop skills, but also strategies and approaches. In this course the processes of learning were related to purposes, and outcomes were reviewed to provide an indication of the relative success of the strategy adopted. One of the great difficulties for pupils, however, is that such 'learning to learn' workshops are provided outside the normal curriculum. Unless class teachers are prepared systematically to relate the workshops to their own subjects, the effects of such workshops will be slight.

In their work with pupils in primary schools and in the early stages of secondary school, Nisbet and Shucksmith[70] suggest a set of six strategies generally required to complete school tasks effectively (see Table 4.1). Teachers often believe that such strategies are taught, but if so it is generally in an unsystematic way applied only to individual subjects. Some pupils develop very effective study strategies without help from teachers, but others waste time and effort through not even recognising that strategies are required. Learning for them is taken for granted: they have not reflected on their own active role in monitoring and evaluating their own processes of learning. Developing this awareness is a first step in allowing the student to take more responsibility for learning.

For some theorists, however, this type of support does not go far enough. It is still too closely linked to the conventional view of education in which the teacher controls the content and the processes of learning. A more radical view is put forward by Laurie

Table 4.1 A list of commonly mentioned strategies (from J. D. Nisbet and J. Shucksmith (1986) *Learning Strategies*, Routledge and Kegan Paul).

(a) Asking questions:	defining hypotheses, establishing aims and parameters of a task, discovering audience, relating task to previous work, etc.
(b) Planning:	deciding on tactics and timetables, reduction of task or problem into components: what physical or mental skills are necessary?
(c) Monitoring:	continuous attempt to match efforts, answers and discoveries to initial questions or purposes
(d) Checking:	preliminary assessment of performance and results
(e) Revising:	may be simple re-drafting or re-calculation or may involve setting of revised goals
(f) Self-testing:	final self-assessment both of results and performance on task

Thomas and Sheila Harri-Augstein.[99] They have experimented with techniques which draw attention to the ways in which we make sense of the world around us. Our understanding depends on our own idiosyncratic concept structure. Education often seems to attempt to impose a common conceptualisation, and in some areas this may be essential. But there are also advantages in helping students to reflect on the differences between their own interpretations of the world and those of the teacher or of other students. This reflection goes beyond the monitoring of learning strategies to the nature of knowledge itself – in fact back to Marton's 'alternative' view of knowledge. Thomas and Harri-Augstein suggest that learning depends on 'conversations', on negotiations of personal meaning, which lead to understanding. These conversations can be internal, but they are particularly effective when external negotiation of meaning is carried out in pairs or groups. In such situations differing ways of interpreting experience can be explored with mutual benefit. These techniques encourage reflection on the processes of learning as a first step towards becoming a self-organised learner:

Self-organisation in learning arises out of the ability to converse with oneself about the processes of learning; and to observe, search, analyse, formulate, reflect and review on the basis of such encounters . . . Reflecting in context upon one's own experience integrates the results of education . . . into the developing life experience of the individual. The cumulative pool of experience available for reflection is enriched when a person allows the curiosity which arises naturally out of their wishes, needs, thoughts and feelings, to drive their actions. Experience is enriched by exploration and experiment. It is also enriched by entering more fully into the experience of others. Empathising as completely as possible with another's reconstruction of personal events and exploring these . . . in detail and in depth . . . [adds] to one's own personal experience . . . People differ in their ability to learn from experience. They differ in how they select, construct and reflect upon their experience so that they may learn from it. [Yet] each of us can learn to be more sensitive to relevant events. We can take more care in attributing meaning to them, and . . . spend more time reflecting upon our experiences . . . (as well as creating) experiences from which to learn' (pages 3, 15, 17).[99]

Styles of Learning and Teaching

The emphasis on helping pupils to develop personal meaning by reflecting on their experiences takes us back to Carl Rogers and the radical reforms he has proposed in traditional education. Throughout this chapter there has been a gradual shift from teacher control towards a greater pupil responsibility. Which particular method appeals to an individual teacher will depend on the personality and cognitive style of that teacher. It could be argued that

. . . our approaches to teaching reflect previous experiences with learning. We teach as we prefer to learn. Stemming from this is perhaps the most insistent message derived from the research literature. There can be no single 'right' way to study or 'best' way to teach. People differ so much in intellectual abilities, attitudes, and personality that they adopt characteristically different approaches to learning, to teaching, to conducting research, or to writing a book. No one of these approaches could be 'right' for more than a small proportion of people. Yet many teachers and educationalists still proclaim the over-riding merits of one particular philosophy of teaching, and roundly denounce the alternatives. Why should that be? [It seems] . . . that a teacher's strong preference for one or other teaching approach – say formal rather than informal – is a reflection of his own learning style and personality. In one way that is not unreasonable: he may teach best using that approach. But best for whom? Presumably only for those pupils or students who share the teacher's own style of learning. For many others that way of presenting knowledge may create unnecessary difficulties (page 4).[36]

It was Gordon Pask's research, described in Chapter 3, which most clearly demonstrated experimentally how matching teaching with learning styles improved academic performance. But do contrasting teaching styles in actual classrooms similarly affect pupils' learning? To some extent at least, formal methods of teaching represent a serialist style. They are certainly likely to emphasise teacher control, and may also be associated with other characteristics which, taken together, would represent a distinctive style associated with underlying personality. George Leith[64] has contrasted what he sees to be the defining characteristics of formal and informal teachers:

Among [those who adopted] the more formal teaching methods, . . . teachers . . . had been remarked to be conscientious, attentive to detail, impersonal and well organised, while . . . [informal teachers] . . . were characterised by readiness to switch attention and divert to something of immediate interest, concern for global effects rather than precise detail and dislike of tight organisation schedules. The former valued orderliness, obedience to rules, attentiveness, timetable regularity, desks arranged in rows and so on, while the latter preferred spontaneity of responding, enthusiasm, individuality of contribution, no timetable limitations and informal seating (page 16).

These descriptions parallel quite closely, the definitions of serialist and holist styles, and also the poles of the teacher/student control dimension. Various research studies have indicated that formal and informal methods have differential effects.[4,95,102] Informal methods are likely to improve the motivation, and so the attainment, of less able children. They will also be enjoyed more by confident extraverted children. But these methods seem to increase levels of anxiety and depress the attainment level of highly anxious children. It follows that neither extreme formal nor extreme informal methods are likely to suit more than a proportion of any class – those who find that particular style of teaching congenial.

> It is a gross oversight of available knowledge in psychology to assume that looser structure in the environment of the classroom is of some benefit for all children, just because it is of great benefit for some children. It is predictable that children who have a low tolerance for ambiguity and uncertainty would find an open classroom that operates very successfully for some children, extremely threatening and anxiety-provoking. It is also predictable that personality configurations among administrators and teachers who seek out the challenge of innovation in developing the open classroom would tend to be unmindful of the valid needs for order, predictability, and specificity for persons unlike themselves . . . Where open classrooms are established as a schoolwide policy without offering a choice, they are an invitation to disappointment. Without *individual* selection for one programme or the other, and freedom to move back and forth on the basis of experience, it can almost be forecast that there would probably be as many children who lose as there are those who gain (page 467).[50]

The implications of this line of thinking would be that teachers should not adopt too extreme a style – either holist or serialist. Their methods should include sufficient structure and detail to support serialist and anxious pupils, but also enough illustrations and opportunities for personal expression and discussion to accommodate the holist and the extravert. Where feasible, it would also be advantageous to allow pupils to choose styles of learning which suit them, with pupils being helped to recognise their own learning style.

The provision of variety in teaching seems to be a noncontroversial aim. But to match learning style with instructional methods creates a problem. Is it desirable for pupils who have developed an unbalanced reliance on one or other style of learning to be encouraged to rely even more on that style? Should we not be helping them to develop both styles – to make them more versatile? That depends on the source of these differences in style. If they represent differential inherited strengths of the cerebral hemispheres, as Sperry argues, it may be right to play to the strengths. But the assumption of fixed attributes, if applied rigidly to learning style, could become as restricting as it became in relation to general intelligence. Teachers have to look, first, for modifiability.

In Chapter 2 we also heard Sperry claiming that education was one-sidedly emphasising left hemisphere functions. But if the different preferred teaching styles reflect contrasting cerebral dominance in the teacher, then education cannot be as one-sided as Sperry suggests. Its curriculum clearly leans towards the left brain, but some teachers express their cognitive individuality by using methods which rely more on right hemisphere functions. It would seem that different subject areas also utilise more of one or other of the hemispheres. Music, art and movement, together with some aspects of the humanities, would evoke right hemisphere thinking, while languages, sciences and mathematics are dominated by left hemisphere functions.

The demand to encourage right hemisphere thinking in subjects which dominate our main academic curriculum can be seen to parallel an earlier movement to encourage creativity and divergent thinking. It is probably the same demand, but arrived at from different evidence. The safest conclusion seems to be that pupils should be offered opportunities through choice of subjects, topics and learning styles to follow their cerebral strength, but they should also be encouraged to explore the less developed cognitive processes without undue pressure to change their preferences.

Teachers themselves can be expected to have dominant ways of thinking which will influence their ways of teaching. Again it is sensible to encourage them to play to their cerebral strengths. However, there is a tendency for cerebral imbalance to be reflected in strong beliefs about the universal efficacy of their own style of teaching. 'Seminars are the *only* way we can expect students to learn; lectures are useless.' This was a comment from a fellow lecturer which puzzled me at the time. On reflection it seemed that he was really saying '*I* learned best from seminars', yet he was trying to insist that this was a general experience. It is surprising just how strongly some teachers believe that a learning style which is comfortable for them will suit everyone else. That belief is patently false. To avoid such complacency, it is important for teachers to reflect on their own teaching style. Does it provide sufficient balance between holistic and serialist modes of thinking to support the learning of the differing individuals in the class? Could more use be made of visual and auditory stimulation to provoke more effective use of both hemispheres?

One attempt to develop such a system has been reported by Colin Rose.[88] He has brought together a range of techniques, which have been shown to work separately, into a system called *Accelerated Learning*. Currently it is being used for learning foreign languages at home, but he sees applications in education and training more widely. The system involves using relaxation techniques initially to achieve a receptive frame of mind. The language material is presented initially in the form of dramatic scenes and then repeated as a background with baroque music in the foreground. Learners are encouraged to record their own pronunciation and to visualise the scenes. In particular, they are shown how to use striking illustrations to create strong visual associations with new words. Finally, games are used to provoke greater involvement and activity in the learning process.

Variants of this system have proved remarkably successful in various countries, and one of them has been adopted nationally within the Finnish education system. *Accelerated Learning* provides a systematic procedure for helping pupils more effectively to utilise and integrate their various sensory modes and contrasting cerebral functions.

Summary

Methods for managing learning have also been suggested in previous chapters. Thus the ideas presented here should be considered in conjunction with the earlier suggestions of Skinner, Ausubel and Bruner. To return to Figure 1.1, a more coherent view of the differing theories and their implications can be seen.

In this chapter implications for managing classroom learning have been derived mainly from classroom-based research, although computer-based learning and mastery learning have different origins. Both have their roots in programmed learning, but the wide variety of applications of micro-computers now draws on ideas from information-processing and artificial intelligence. Computers offer modes of learning previously not available to teachers, but the effects of differing programming modes on children's learning are still far from clear.

Mastery learning provides a way of organising classroom learning which takes account of intellectual differences. Emphasising mastery requirements, and providing time to reach mastery, changes the classroom climate considerably. Time spent on task clearly has important influences on how much pupils learn. And the way teachers organise their classroom and the curriculum will affect the time their pupils have available for learning. However, it is also important for teachers to understand how pupils develop under-standing – what procedures they follow. Task analysis is providing valuable insights into pupils' ways of constructing understanding, as well as the ways in which they try to make sense of the reward system operating in the classroom.

Approaches to learning are influenced by assessment procedures, by dependency on the teacher, by the time available, and by the quality of teaching. Techniques have been devised to help pupils to become more aware of their own learning strategies, and also to reflect on their own experience. Thus a deep approach depends on the teacher providing a suitable context and the pupils taking more responsibility for their own learning strategies.

Finally a teacher's own personality and cognitive style will lead to a preference for a particular style of teaching. Formal and informal methods seem to parallel the earlier descriptions of contrasting learning styles. It is thus important for teachers to avoid adopting too extreme a style which will create learning difficulties for pupils with the opposite learning style.

5

Understanding and Influencing Classroom Learning

The previous chapters have introduced a varied selection of ideas about learning and how it can be effectively managed within classroom contexts. That variety can be explained in part by the undeveloped state of social science research compared with the physical or biological sciences. There is little doubt that the explanations of classroom learning suggested by psychologists will gain in precision and practical utility as new research techniques are developed. But it is likely that even a new generation of learning theories will retain inherent contradictions related both to the experience and training of the theorists, and to their beliefs about the nature of education.

The behaviourists and their successors have used analogies which relate education to a production system. If that system can be described accurately enough and its components specified, the learning processes can then be controlled to ensure a satisfactory product. Social engineering is at the heart of behaviourist thinking. But education is like life itself – both social and personal. It is to be expected that each society should be very concerned about the knowledge, skills, behaviour, and attitudes of its future citizens. The state, to differing degrees, will control the education system and determine individuals' access to knowledge. It may even lay down a defined syllabus and rules for how it should be taught. But every individual views the opportunities provided by the education system in different ways, and so the teachers and students involved all have differing perceptions of education and the learning process. And the way anybody behaves is a product not just of the situation, but of that person's *perception* of the situation. In turn, the perception depends on previous experience and on the personal characteristics of the individual. If education is viewed from this perspective, the analogy of a production system becomes entirely inappropriate. An alternative analogy has to be sought.

Biological analogies have likened education to the growth of a plant, determined partly genetically and partly by nutrients and environment. But even this analogy misses the essential fact that a human being is conscious of the processes involved in learning and interacts with the environment, even changing that environment. The experiential psychologists develop this argument to the point where the student may take over responsibility for, and control of, learning. Within a State education system, however, such a radical approach is unlikely to be acceptable.

It is probably safer to move away from distant analogies and to seek instead a model which brings together important factors which have been shown to influence classroom learning. Such a model should not be drawn from either extreme of the range of learning theories, if it is to be widely acceptable and practicable. Nor should it be narrowly prescriptive. Instead it should provide a framework to guide a teacher's thinking in relation to a particular classroom context. What we require is thus a *heuristic* model of classroom learning.

A Heuristic Model of Classroom Learning

How then can the complexity of the classroom be represented in a way which may be more useful to teachers? Any model in a book is necessarily static, yet it must at least imply the dynamic characteristics of the classroom. It can do that by drawing attention to the factors which most directly influence classroom learning, and to the ways in which those factors are likely to interact. Above all, the model needs to be 'emancipatory': it must draw the attention of the teacher to what can be changed. Which factors are most directly under the control of the teacher or school, and which are dependent on the pupils or their home and peer group backgrounds? The model should also indicate the limitations on teacher influence – how the pupils' individual perceptions filter the effects of the environment. Thus we need a model which hints at change and restrains any suggestion of total teacher control through a recognition of pupil responsibility and individuality. The teacher is seen as influencing, but not determining, learning. In total that represents a daunting set of demands. Any model incorporating such requirements will be complex, but there should still be a simplifying pattern to retain a recognisable representation of reality.

In developing such a model a balance has to be sought between completeness and simplicity. Too much detail creates confusion, and yet the model has to provide an accurate description of a complex social reality. The basic components of the model will be concepts identified by research which are also, as far as possible, part of, or relatable to, a teacher's professional vocabulary. In this way the ideas within the model will be more readily understood. Of course, the underlying definitions of the research-based concepts should also be borne in mind.

The model can be used as a summary of some of the main concepts and ideas introduced in earlier chapters. But its main function is to encourage teachers to examine their own classroom learning context within a framework which guides their thinking but does not prescribe actions. Because it brings together the influences on learning of the pupil's own characteristics, and also of parents, peers, teachers and school, the model provides no general prescriptions about teaching or learning. Nor are they desirable. Researchers should not seek to make general prescriptions. Decisions about teaching and learning have to be left to those who can interpret the specific conditions within an individual classroom.

Outline of the model

Although the model has been developed out of concepts and relationships derived from empirical studies, the evidence is far from complete. The model must thus be expected to change, as evidence accumulates. At present, some of the relationships suggested in the model can be justified directly by the research findings, some depend on analogies or parallels with related concepts, while others represent logical deductions from defining features of the concepts. At first sight the model will probably seem over-elaborate and confusing. However, if the general structure is considered first, before examining how the individual elements fit into each part of the overall pattern, the diagram should become easier to understand.

One of the basic premises underlying the development of the model was that no single way of presenting information or one method of teaching would be equally suitable for all pupils. The range and variety of individual differences affecting learning make that impossible. The idea of aptitude-treatment interaction (Chapter 1), of matching teaching to the learner provides an ideal. But both the terminology and the assumptions of this approach are suitable only for the controlled environment of the psychological laboratory. It is impossible within the classroom to think of single aptitudes or narrowly defined instructional methods (treatments). A range of both individual differences and environmental influences have to be considered simultaneously in trying to understand the efficacy of differing classroom procedures.

The model had its origins in research on student learning[38] and was developed in stages. The first step was to define the major influences on what pupils learn. These are taken to be the teacher, the school, the home and peer group, and the individual pupil. In the model itself (Figure 5.1), these four main influences are placed in the four corners, while the central 'diamond' focuses attention on to learning processes and strategies and outcomes of learning. Within this diamond are placed a series of broad concepts which have been shown to have a direct influence on how pupils learn – skill in learning, attitude to education, approach to learning, learning tasks, knowledge base, and skill in teaching.

At the centre of the model are the learning processes and strategies, and the outcomes of learning, which are to be explained in terms of the other components within the model. Processes and outcomes are influenced from above by the personal characteristics of the pupil and by parental support and peer group pressures, and from below by the teacher and the school. Between these two sets of influences lie the pupil's perceptions of the learning situation. The teacher is responsible for selecting appropriate content matter from the knowledge base (taken also to include skills and attitudes) and presenting it, either directly or through selected resource material, to the pupil. The teacher helps the pupil to perceive meaning and relevance in the knowledge presented, and also sets a variety of

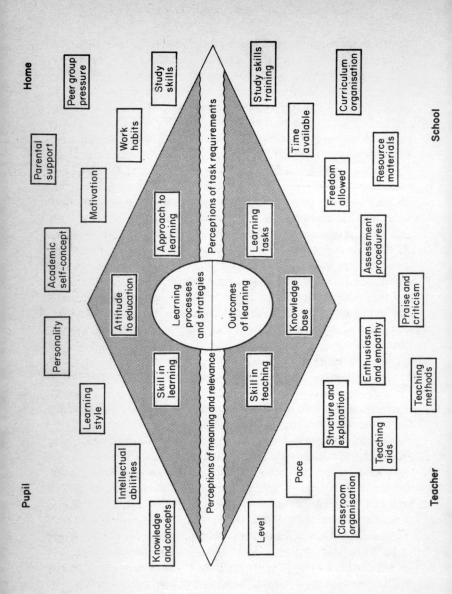

Figure 5.1 A heuristic model of the teaching-learning process

learning tasks, the requirements of which have to be interpreted by the pupil. These two main forms of perception play a mediating role, indicated by the wavy lines across the centre of the model. It is the individual perceptions of the situations, rather than the situations themselves, which are taken to influence learning processes and outcomes.

The main concepts used to describe the pupil characteristics are skill in learning, approach to learning, and attitudes to education. Approaches to learning contain within their defining features both intentions (to reach personal understanding or simply to complete task requirements) and contrasting learning processes associated with those opposite intentions. But the ability to carry out a deep approach depends on previous knowledge and intellectual abilities, and the way it is carried out depends on personality and learning style. This combination of individual characteristics has been called 'skill in learning', being broader than the term 'ability'. Attitudes towards education indicate towards what ends the educational opportunities provided in the school are being directed. These attitudes are linked to the academic self-concept and motivation, and are strongly influenced by parents and peer group. Variations in approach to learning can be attributed, in part, to differences in the level and direction of motivation, in work habits, and in study skills. These concepts are not seen as describing basic psychological characteristics of the pupil: they are more immediately influenced by both home and school environments.

In the bottom half of the model, the term 'skill in teaching' is again used broadly, this time to describe the teacher's influence on the pupil's learning. By teaching, and by choosing materials and tasks, the teacher is controlling the level and pace of presentation of knowledge. Teaching also depends on providing a structure and a set of explanations which are presented with varying degrees of enthusiasm and empathy. Teachers also influence learning through their use of praise and criticism. Different classroom organisation, teaching aids and teaching methods may reflect different teaching styles, but they also introduce additional influences on learning.

The learning tasks that the teacher selects are constrained by characteristics of the school – the available resource materials and the curriculum organisation. The factors which have been found most directly to influence approaches to learning are assessment procedures, the relative freedom or independence allowed in learning, time available (or workload), and provision of study skills training. The teacher may have some control over these factors, but they are also dependent on school policies reflected in the general curriculum organisation. The specific learning tasks presented in the classroom will be reinterpreted by the pupils in terms of the more general learning context provided by the school.

Having provided an initial overview of the structure of the model, its components will now be examined in more detail. If teachers are to be able to make practical use of this model, not only must the concepts be clearly understood, but ways of recognising different levels or categories within them will also have to be made explicit.

Descriptions of the pupil

The upper left-hand part of the model, describing *skill in teaching* indicates those pupil characteristics which are considered to be relatively stable, being rooted in a combination of extensive past experience and physiological or neurological differences. This is not to suggest that these characteristics are unalterable, but that only under unusual conditions will sudden changes of level or type be found.

Within this model the outcomes of learning are seen as including *academic knowledge and skills*, some of which will be appropriately absorbed in a relatively unreflective way at first. Greater importance is, however, placed on the way this body of knowledge is subsequently reorganised and structured to achieve personal understanding. And outcomes will also involve the development of practical, social, and interpersonal skills. This body of knowledge and skills will be immeasurably strengthened if it is taught in ways which ensure that it is firmly rooted in the real-world experiences of pupils. Some topics, in their more abstract formulations, necessarily remain separate intellectual microworlds, but a great deal of academic knowledge is intended to provide useful representations of the real world. Too often the way in which examination syllabuses and courses are organised prevents experiential linkages being established, and forces academic knowledge into separate and remote corners of the mind which are rarely revisited.

Ausubel argued (see Chapter 2), that the single most important piece of information a teacher could have was a clear idea of the current state of knowledge of the pupil. Although it may be useful to assess that knowledge in conventional ways, based on tests of discrete pieces of information, teachers really need to know a great deal more about the way pupils are conceptualising each main topic area. One way of 'tapping' a pupil's cognitive structure is to use concept maps, as Novak recommended (Chapter 2). But conventional written work can also be used, if it is assessed in terms of the SOLO taxonomy (Chapter 2) to draw the teacher's attention to the quality of thinking involved and the level of understanding reached.

If objective tests are used to provide an indication of *intellectual abilities*, it is important not to rely solely on verbal reasoning. Broader based tests should be used to reflect the existence of 'multiple intelligences', such as those described by Gardner (Chapter 1). If possible, tests tapping spatial abilities and intellectual flexibility should be included, but if time is limited the *Passage 10–13*[55] provides a minimum profile, with scores on communication skills, mathematics and reasoning for the 10–12 age group. The techniques of mastery learning suggest one way in which general intellectual differences can be handled without socially divisive labelling and grouping policies. But in secondary schools, flexible ability grouping or setting can be used to take account of specific abilities, and it may be essential to adopt it in some subject areas. Variations in intellectual skills may be so marked that effective classroom teaching or management become difficult, even impossible, for all but a small minority of exceptional teachers. Intellectual stimulation and competition is increasingly being recognised as essential for the most able children,[30] even if this is provided for only part of their time in school.

Within the model, the teaching component of 'level' is placed immediately below previous knowledge, while 'pace' is under intellectual abilities: this positioning indicates a logical connection between them. Similarly, the degree of structure and the nature of explanations provided should be seen in relation to pupils' *learning styles*. The simplest formulation of these differences reflects the contrasting functions attributed to the two cerebral hemispheres. The term 'holist' has been used to indicate a strong preference for adopting a broad view of learning, with an impulsive willingness to see similarities between ideas and a preference for strong imagery in building up idiosyncratic meaning. 'Serialist' implies a narrow focus, a cautious concern with differences or evidence which does not fit: it also involves a preference for logical organisation and meaning developed through formal definitions and concrete examples. This type of narrow focus should be distinguished from the surface approach in which the focus is controlled by the specific task requirements. If time and assessment constraints allow, an initial serialist focus can broaden to link evidence to ideas, and ideas to experience in ways which develop deeper understanding. But in practice a serialist style often becomes indistinguishable from a surface approach because the initial attention to detail may be perceived by the pupil as being all that is required by the teacher.

Teachers may find it particularly difficult to recognise the contrasting learning styles, as the more readily observable personality traits may dominate. By careful questioning about class work and by observing the way materials are used in project work, indications of holist and serialist styles may, however, be obtained. It is possible to supplement these observations with self-report inventories or questionnaires. An inventory to cover all the non-intellectual characteristics contained in the model is currently being developed (see Appendix). Used as a basis for discussion with the pupil, and as a focus for further observation, responses to the questions can provide the teacher with a more systematic picture of personal characteristics which influence learning.

It is through the relationships established with a class that teachers express their personalities. Enthusiasm and empathy are the characteristics of teaching shown directly under *personality* within the model. But from the research findings, it is clear that different teaching methods affect differentially pupils with contrasting personalities. Extraverts and pupils low in anxiety are more likely to enjoy classrooms emphasising collaborative group work and discussions. Introverts need time to work quietly on their own, to find things out for themselves, and they may well enjoy competition. Anxious pupils are comfortable neither in an open classroom nor in a competitive situation. They need the emotional warmth associated with the best informal methods, but combined with a degree of structure and predictability more often linked with formal methods. Yet formal assessment procedures induce anxiety and fear of failure. There is a difficult balance to be achieved here.

Teachers recognise extraversion, and particularly aggressive extraversion, readily: it impinges directly on them. But anxious introverts merge into their surroundings, avoid attention, and may not be given sufficient attention, particularly in a large class. Estimates of the strength of these personality traits can be obtained by using Eysenck's *Junior Personality Questionnaire*[46] or the sub-scales of social extraversion and fear of failure of the inventory described in the Appendix.

Influence of the home

The pupil characteristics shown in the top right-hand part of the model are considered to be more readily modifiable by experience. Teachers, parents and peer groups all play important roles in influencing pupils' self-concepts, motivation, and work habits – as indicated by Burns in Chapter 3. The importance of the general attitude, or orientation, towards education in affecting specific reactions to individual courses was also stressed in Chapter 3. This attitude is, of course, strongly influenced by *parents and peer groups*, but also represents a personal evaluation of the likely benefits of educational experiences. The course and the knowledge base can be seen extrinsically in narrowly vocational or instrumental terms as providing solely a path towards qualifications and career. Alternatively they can be viewed as providing potentially useful knowledge and opportunities for intellectual and personal development.

Teachers generally see their subject as intrinsically interesting and relevant to life or culture, but many pupils see it at best as having only extrinsic value or at worst as having little or no relevance to the world they meet outside the school. In the model, *attitude to education* is used to reflect pupils' perceptions of the combination of content, teaching and school. This attitude is seen as a powerful influence on the amount of effort applied to the differing learning processes and so is closely associated with learning outcomes.

Approach to learning is a concept which brings together pupils' intentions and the processes used to fulfil those intentions. It helps teachers to understand the ways in which pupils tackle the learning tasks given to them. Approach depends mainly on previous experiences of learning, in particular on what types of learning are rewarded, and in what ways, by teachers and parents. The residual effects of these experiences can be described in terms of the predominant motivational pattern of the pupil. And the teacher provides within the classroom a new set of experiences of rewards and punishments (or criticisms) which shape future motivation and behaviour.

In Chapter 3, three distinct forms of *motivation* were identified – intrinsic motivation, fear of failure, and need for achievement. And these different forms of motivation were found to be closely associated with contrasting intentions and approaches to learning – deep, surface, and strategic, respectively. It is not sufficient, therefore, to ask teachers to develop motivation. Different learning tasks and assessment practices will reinforce different types of motivation. Extrinsic rewards will push pupils towards strategic, surface approaches, with unintended consequences for pupil learning.

A crucially important role of the teacher involves motivating the pupil to learn. Many of the traditional techniques (gold stars, house points, and even marks themselves) emphasise competition and present extrinsic rewards. How can the teacher create intrinsic motivation in ways which will have a knock-on effect on attitudes, self-concept, and work habits? Jere Brophy, a well-known American researcher, has recently developed a list of teacher activities designed to develop student motivation.[17] These are summarised in Table 5.1. Brophy suggests that teachers aim to use the first three general strategies in all lessons, and also to try to include one or more of the other strategies when introducing the topic, managing classroom activities, and assigning follow-up work. Above all, Brophy emphasises the need for teachers to spend more time and care in explaining the relevance and potential interest of each topic or task before setting pupils to work – otherwise pupils engage in 'busy work' and their goal is limited to completing the task to the satisfaction of the teacher using a variety of ploys to avoid real interaction with the content.

Another important theme stressed by Brophy, and running through the earlier chapters, is the need to help pupils become more aware of their own learning processes. Teachers have tended to overemphasise **content** to the exclusion of **process**. Pupils need to be shown how to learn. Teachers need to model clear thinking, memory strategies, and problem-solving, by showing how they do it themselves and in particular indicating the way difficulties can be overcome. Teachers have a wealth of experience of general

Table 5.1 Strategies for motivating (adapted from J. Brophy (forth-coming) 'Socialising student motivation to learn' in M. L. Maehr and D. A. Kleiber (eds) *Advances in Motivation and Achievement (Volume 5)*, JAI Press)

General strategies
1 Stress value and relevance of school work to everyday life
2 Show that you expect pupils to enjoy learning
3 Treat tests as ways of checking personal progress

Specific strategies
4 Explain why you find a topic or idea interesting
5 Introduce topics or tasks in ways which arouse interest
6 Create suspense or stimulate curiosity
7 Make abstract content more personal, concrete or familiar
8 Present paradoxes or incongruities for discussion
9 Encourage pupils to relate topics to their own interests
10 Explain course objectives and help pupils set their own goals and targets
11 Provide full and informative feedback on performance
12 Teach problem-solving by personal example
13 Encourage metacognitive awareness of learning processes (provide and discuss memory aids, and lead group discussions on alternative learning strategies)

strategies of learning, but only rarely are they discussed openly and explicitly with the class.

Motivation is not simply a characteristic of the pupil. It is very much a pupil's reaction both to past experiences of home and earlier schooling, and to the current set of learning experiences. As Kozéki has argued (Chapter 1), the teacher has the responsibility not only of increasing levels of motivation, but also providing an appropriate range of different types of reward to accommodate differing motivational styles (emotional, cognitive and moral). In dealing with individual pupils it may also be necessary to help create a more balanced motivational style as part of more general personality development.

Academic self-concept, or self-esteem within the school, depends on teachers' comments both in class and on returned work. Somehow the teacher has to strike a balance between objectivity, fairness, and encouragement. Pupils have a fairly clear idea of the relative worth of their work, so unqualified praise is unlikely to be effective. The comments need to value effort and suggest specific ways in which better results could be achieved. Teachers' comments are often too vague to help pupils towards specific improvements. The use of diagnostic assessments, making use of the power of microcomputers, was suggested in Chapter 4 as a way of providing specific feedback. But encouragement and personal regard remain the province of the teacher in developing a positive self-concept in the pupil.

Academic self-concept is just one facet of general self-esteem. If esteem is uniformly low, it may seriously interfere with all a pupil's activities. Carl Rogers (Chapter 1) wanted teachers to show empathy, unconditional positive regard, and genuineness, as a way of boosting pupil self-concept. In clinical therapy this is much easier to achieve than in a classroom environment. Robert Burns[23] has a range of more specific and practical suggestions to offer. For example, he describes the use of positive thinking exercises and visualisation of success. People with poor self-images tend to dwell on difficulties and disappointments, yet everyone experiences limited success. It is possible to help pupils look for the more positive aspects of their work and social activities and to imagine what a more successful outcome would be like. Such activities may be of considerable general benefit to children who lack parental support or who lack self-confidence.

Work habits and study methods, as well as specific skills and strategies develop as an interaction between the influence of school, home, and peer group. Work habits at home, and in particular the time spent on studying or educational pursuits out of school, depend crucially on the parents. Without opportunities to work quietly and, in the earlier years, parental insistence on an appropriate balance between work and leisure, the effort of the teacher may be wasted. Effective time management seems to come naturally to some pupils, but others need to be taught such skills. In the previous chapter it was argued that courses, like that described by Ian Selmes in *Improving Study Skills*,[90] could be developed to help pupils develop not just the basic skills of studying but also ways of relating processes to purposes. This is how pupils can be encouraged to become effective learners.

they are intended to facilitate. For what specific purpose is a particular teaching aid being used? Little use of teaching aids leads to a rather monotonous instructional diet, but it is also possible to interfere with learning by an over-reliance on them. Pupils can only attend to one sense at a time: visual illustrations and auditory commentary need to carry the same message or they will interfere. And thorough preparation and 'debriefing' are necessary if radio or television programmes are being introduced into the curriculum. Without follow-up work, pupils may treat the programmes as incidental entertainment. They need to know what to look out for, and to have opportunities afterwards to question and discuss.

Teaching methods summarise the classroom organisation and the use of teaching aids, but they also include the typical ways of presenting information. They describe not only the relative reliance on class teaching and the individual or group work by pupils, but also the techniques of questioning, of group discussion, of dramatic simulations, of peer tutoring, and so on. It is impossible even to mention the whole range of methods available across the different school subjects. The intention of the model is to remind teachers of the effect which choices of teaching methods are likely to have on the types of learning pupils adopt, and on their learning outcomes. Methods are needed which not only encourage pupils to seek meaning and relevance, to be active, imaginative and questioning, but also to recognise the need for accuracy and precision. No one method can achieve this ideal: the art of good teaching involves arranging an appropriate variety and emphasis for a particular class and ultimately the individual pupil. The evidence suggests, however, that reliance on formal teaching methods leaves the pupil overdependent on the teacher and unlikely to adopt a deep approach to learning.

Assessment procedures have perhaps the most immediate effect on how and what pupils learn. The school, or the examination board, determines the general procedures, but the teacher retains control over term-time assessment. Through the type of questions asked and the extent and nature of the feedback provided, the pupils are given a strong impression of what the teacher considers to be important and worthwhile. The feedback needs to provide both precise information on what is wrong and how it can be put right, and also encouragement or fair criticism. It is particularly valuable to discuss pupils' mistakes with them. As Charles Desforges suggested (Chapter 4), such informal information helps teachers to understand the nature and sources of pupils' difficulties. Praise and blame, together with marks and comments, are the currency of classroom interactions between teacher and pupil. Their importance cannot be overestimated. No amount of exhortation can counteract the influence of assessment rewards if they are in a different direction. Questions and answers in class and in tests provide the most potent way of influencing learning: they model, as Ference Marton argued in Chapter 4, the teacher's own conception of learning and influence the pupils' decisions about what is important to learn.

The *curriculum organisation* of the school embodies its policies and philosophy. It will determine the *time available* for the different school subjects, it will guide teachers' decisions about teaching methods and the amount of choice and *freedom allowed* to pupils. It will also embody decisions about the provision of *study skills training*. Yet, within that overall organisation, the teacher usually retains important freedom within the classroom to provide opportunities for choice for the pupils, to ensure that time is used productively, to avoid overloading pupils in ways which preclude deep approaches, and to provide help with study strategies and skills specific to a particular subject area or age group.

Using the Model

In relation to this book, the model provides a useful summary of some of the main concepts and relationships discussed in previous chapters. But its main purpose is to draw attention to teaching and learning as a complex interactive process in which the outcomes depend on the school, the teachers, parents, peers and the individual pupil. The model cannot give precise predictions of the outcomes of learning. It is intended to provide guidance to the teacher in thinking about ways of improving the quality and quantity of learning in the classroom. Too often in the past, research studies have recommended changes of one specific aspect of the classroom or of teaching methods without recognising the way other facets of classroom organisation or school policy may interfere with those changes. For example, there has recently been growing interest in helping pupils to 'learn how to learn'. The idea is to provide either special workshops or carefully designed materials for use in normal lessons. But to introduce such additional teaching alongside traditional curricula and teaching methods is unlikely to be successful. The model indicates that study skills training is but one element in the whole pattern of interactions. It should warn the innovator to think carefully about pupils' existing knowledge and to consider whether pupils of all ability levels are to be involved. But above all it should remind teachers that the ability to adopt a deep approach to studying is not just a matter of skill. It depends on motivation, self-concept and attitude on the one hand, and on the reward systems and teaching methods in the school on the other. If the teaching encourages dependency, and if the assessment procedures and teachers' comments reward simple factual responses, no amount of training in metacognitive strategies can override the more powerful and immediate reinforcements occurring in the classroom. The model can thus help teachers think more holistically about teaching and learning within a school and classroom setting.

Inevitably, the particular set of concepts presented within this heuristic model, and the emphasis indicated by the positioning of the concepts, represents the judgement of the author. It also grew out of research into student learning, although supplemented by classroom research. This initial heuristic model will need to evolve as new concepts and research findings are introduced, and it also seems likely that such models will be more helpful if they are made specific to a particular age range or subject area. It should be possible to map holistically the salient features of infant or primary classrooms, of literature or science lessons in secondary schools, of informal adult learning sessions, and of university or college education. This, however, is a challenge for the future. At the moment the importance of the current heuristic model is to provoke a view of teaching and learning which breaks the traditional narrowness of theories of learning generated either in the psychological laboratory or in the tradition of general laws of learning.

An understanding of classroom learning does necessitate knowledge of general principles of learning, of memory and cognitive development, and of the main individual differences in learning processes and styles, but it also demands a recognition of the wide range of contextual influences which affect learning in the real-life setting of the classroom and school.

Summary

The model provided in this final chapter is an attempt to bring together some of the important concepts used to describe influence on classroom learning. These influences include the pupil's own relatively stable psychological characteristics, and also the influences of home, teachers and school. The pupil characteristics can be simplified into skill in learning, attitude to learning, and approach to learning. These interact with the pupils' perceptions of the learning environment which can be summarised in terms of skill in teaching, knowledge base, and learning tasks.

Overall, the model is intended to point up the interactions which occur in learning. It is useless to decide on a method of teaching irrespective of the ethos of the school or the individual characteristics of the pupil. The complex interactions which describe the reality of the classroom cannot be reduced to general learning principles or uniform instructional procedures. Styles of learning differ too much for this to be possible. All that the teacher can provide is a learning environment designed to allow pupils with differing styles to learn effectively. There are, of course, general guidelines of what is likely to be effective teaching, but those guidelines need to be sensitively reinterpreted in relation to each classroom context. And teachers must remain alert to the difficulties and attitudes of pupils to ensure that they are able to modify their strategies appropriately. This alertness is part of the empathy which is the hallmark of the gifted teacher.

Additional Reading

Bennett, S. N. and Desforges, C. W. (1985) (eds) *Recent Advances in Classroom Research*. Edinburgh: Scottish Academic Press. (A set of specially written articles prepared for the *British Journal of Educational Psychology*)

Entwistle, N. J. (1985) (ed.) *New Directions in Educational Psychology: I – Learning and Teaching*. Lewes: Falmer Press. (A set of articles covering many of the areas discussed in this book – some specially written, some reprints of earlier articles)

Entwistle, N. J. (1981) *Styles of Learning and Teaching*. London: John Wiley & Sons Ltd. (A more advanced textbook presenting evidence and theories in more detail and with wider coverage)

Appendix

Typical Inventory Items to Measure Various Pupil Characteristics

(designed for use with older pupils in secondary schools)

Approaches to Learning

Deep approach
— I often ask myself questions about what I'm reading or what we are told in class.
— I generally put a lot of effort into trying to understand things which initially seem difficult.
— In trying to understand new ideas, I often try to relate them to real life situations.

Surface approach
— I find I have to rely a good deal on learning things by heart.
— When I'm trying to remember something, I try to imagine the order in which it came in class.
— Often I find I have to read things without having a chance really to understand them.

Strategic approach
— When I'm doing a piece of work, I try to work out how to get the highest possible marks on it.

— I try to work out what the teachers are looking for when they give marks.
— I take care to prevent my social or personal life interfering with my studying.

Learning Styles

Holist
— I enjoy doing things where I can use my imagination or my own ideas.
— Ideas in books often set me off on long trains of thought or produce pictures in my mind.
— When I'm trying to remember something, I can often see or hear it in my mind.

Serialist
— I generally prefer to go through a problem one step at a time.
— I prefer teachers to present things in a clear and well organised way, even if the lessons are not all that interesting.
— I find it difficult to 'switch tracks' when I'm working something out: I keep along the same lines until I'm sure it won't work.

Work Habits

Study methods
— I almost always look through my work carefully before handing it in.
— I often add my own notes to those we have taken in class.
— It's not often that I leave revision until the last minute.

Time Management
— I organise my study time carefully to make the most of it.
— I'm usually prompt at starting work in the evening.
— It's most unusual for me to be late in handing in work.

Motivation

Intrinsic
— I really enjoy a good deal of my school work.
— There are a lot of lessons which I find really interesting.
— I sometimes follow up things we are doing at school in my own time.

Fear of failure
— I worry a good deal about whether I shall be able to cope with new work that we meet.
— I often seem to panic in an exam, so that my mind goes blank.
— I often lie awake worrying about something I've done or said, or something that's coming up next day.

Need for achievement
— I enjoy competition in school work: it makes me work better.
— It generally annoys me a good deal to get lower marks than I expect.
— It's important to me to get better marks than my friends, if I possibly can.

Personality

Social extraversion
— I like to be in the swim of things: if there is anything going on I like to be there.
— I rarely feel shy, even when I meet people for the first time.
— When there's a discussion, I usually manage to join in easily enough.

Academic self-concept
— I seem to manage quite well with most of my school work.
— I can usually pick out the important points in a lesson or what I read.
— I seem to be able to get my ideas over well enough.

References and Bibliography

1 **Ausubel, D. P., Novak, J. S.** and **Hanesian, H.** (1978) *Educational Psychology: a Cognitive View* (2nd Ed.). New York: Holt, Rinehart and Winston.
2 **Badger, E.** (1981) 'Why aren't girls better at maths?', *Educational Research*, 24, 11–23.
3 **Barnes, D.** (1969) *Language, the Learner, and the School.* Harmondsworth: Penguin Books.
4 **Bennett, S. N.** (1976) *Teaching Styles and Pupil Progress.* London: Open Books.
5 **Bennett, S. N.** (1985) 'Time and teach: teaching-learning processes in primary school' in **Entwistle, N. J.** (ed.) *New Directions in Educational Psychology – Learning and Teaching.* Lewes: Falmer Press.
6 **Bennett, S. N.** (1985) 'Interaction and achievement in classroom groups' in **Bennett, S. N.** and **Desforges, C. W.** (eds) *Recent Advances in Classroom Research.* Edinburgh: Scottish Academic Press.
7 **Bennett, S. N., Andreae, J., Hegarty, P.** and **Wade, B.** (1980) *Open Plan Schools: Teaching, Curriculum and Design.* Windsor: NFER.
8 **Bennett, S. N., Desforges, C. W., Cockburn, A. D.** and **Wilkinson, B.** (1984) *The Quality of Pupil Learning Experience.* London: Lawrence Erlbaum.
9 **Biggs, J. B.** and **Collis, K. E.** (1982) *Evaluating the Quality of Learning: the Solo Taxonomy.* New York: Academic Press.
10 **Birney, R. C., Birdick, H.** and **Teevan, R. C.** (1969) *Fear of Failure.* New York: Van Nostrand Reinhold.
11 **Block, J. H.** (1974) (ed.) *Schools, Society and Mastery Learning.* New York: Holt, Rinehart and Winston.
12 **Block, J. H.** (1985) 'Promoting excellence through mastery learning' in **Entwistle, N. J.** (ed.) *New Directions in Educational Psychology – Learning and Teaching.* Lewes: Falmer Press.
13 **Block, J. H.** and **Burns, R. B.** (1976) 'Mastery Learning' in **Schulman, L.** (ed.) *Review of Research in Education (volume 4).* Itasca, IU: F. E. Peacock.
14 **Bloom, B. S.** (1976) *Human Characteristics and School Learning.* New York: McGraw Hill.
15 **Brand, C. R.** and **Dreary, I. J.** (1982) 'Intelligence and "inspection time"' in **Eysenck, H. J.** (ed.) *A Model for Intelligence.* Berlin: Springer Verlag.
16 **Broadbent, D. E.** (1966) 'The well-ordered mind', *American Educational Research Journal*, 3, 281–95.
17 **Brophy, J.** (forthcoming) 'Socialising student motivation to learn' in **Maehr, M. L.** and **Kleiber, D. A.** (eds) *Advances in Motivation and Achievement (Volume 5).* Greenwich, CT: JAI Press.
18 **Bruner, J. S.** (1960) *The Process of Education.* Cambridge, Mass: Harvard University Press.
19 **Bruner, J. S.** (1966) *Toward a Theory of Instruction.* Cambridge, Mass: Harvard University Press.
20 **Bruner, J. S.** (1974) *Beyond the Information Given.* London: George Allen and Unwin.

21 Bruner, J. S. (1983) *In Search of Mind*. New York: Harper and Row.
22 Burns, R. B. (1979) *The Self-Concept: Theory, Measurement, Development and Behaviour*. London: Longman.
23 Burns, R. B. (1982) *Self-Concept, Development and Education*. London: Holt, Rinehart and Winston.
24 Claxton, G. (1985) 'Experiential learning and education' in Entwistle, N. J. (ed.) *New Directions in Educational Psychology – Learning and Teaching*. Lewes: Falmer Press.
25 Cohen, G. (1983) *The Psychology of Cognition*. London: Academic Press.
26 Cooley, W. W. and Lohner, P. R. (1976) *Evaluation Research in Education*. New York: Irvington Wiley.
27 Covington, M. (1983) 'Motivated cognitions' in Paris, S. G., Olson, G. M. and Stevenson, H. W. (eds) *Learning and Motivation in the Classroom*. Hillsdale, NJ: Lawrence Erlbaum.
28 Cronbach, L. J. (1957) 'The two disciplines of scientific psychology', *American Psychologist*, 12, 671–84.
29 Cronbach, L. J. and Snow, R. E. *Aptitudes and Instructional Methods*. New York: Irvington.
30 Department of Education and Science (1985) *Better Schools*. London: HMSO.
31 Desforges, C. W. (1985) 'Matching tasks to children' in Bennett, S. N. and Desforges, C. W. (eds) *Recent Advances in Classroom Research*. Edinburgh: Scottish Academic Press.
32 Desforges, C. W., Bennett, S. N., Cockburn, A. and Willkinson, B. (1985) 'Understanding the quality of pupil learning experiences' in Entwistle, N. J. (ed.) *New Directions in Educational Psychology – Learning and Teaching*. Lewes: Falmer Press.
33 Donaldson, M. (1978) *Children's Minds*. London: Fontana.
34 Driver, R. M. (1982) 'Children learning science', *Educational Analysis*, 4, 2, 69–79.
35 Entwistle, N. J. (1972) 'Personality and academic attainment', *British Journal of Educational Psychology*, 42, 137–51.
36 Entwistle, N. J. (1981) *Styles of Learning and Teaching*. London: Wiley.
37 Entwistle, N. J. (1984) 'Contrasting Perspectives on Learning' in Marton, F., Hounsell, D. J. and Entwistle, N. J. (eds) *The Experience of Learning*. Edinburgh: Scottish Academic Press.
38 Entwistle, N. J. (forthcoming) in Richardson, J. T. E., Eysenck, M. W. and Warren-Piper, D. (eds) *Student Learning: Research in Education and Cognitive Psychology*. London: SRHE and Open University Press.
39 Entwistle, N. J. and Cunningham, S. (1968) 'Neuroticism and school attainment – a linear relationship?', *British Journal of Educational Psychology*, 38, 137–51.
40 Entwistle, N. J. and Hounsell, D. J. (1975) (eds) *How Students Learn*. University of Lancaster: Institute for Post-Compulsory Education.
41 Entwistle, N. J. and Kozéki, B. (1985) 'Relationships between school motivation, approaches to studying, and attainment among British and Hungarian adolescents', *British Journal of Educational Psychology*, 55, 124–37.
42 Entwistle, N. J. and Ramsden, P. (1983) *Understanding Student Learning*. London: Croom Helm.
43 Entwistle, N. J. and Wilson, J. D. (1977) *Degrees of Excellence: the Academic Achievement Game*. London: Hodder and Stoughton.
44 Eysenck, H. J. (1965) *Fact and Fiction in Psychology*. Harmondsworth: Penguin Books.

45 **Eysenck, H. J.** (1983) 'Heredity and environment: the state of the debate' in **Entwistle, N. J.** (ed.) *New Directions in Educational Psychology – Learning and Teaching.* Lewes: Falmer Press.

46 **Eysenck, H. J.** and **Eysenck, S. B. G.** (1975) *Manual of the Eysenck Personality Questionnaire.* San Diego, Calif: Educational & Industrial Testing Service.

47 **Eysenck, M. W.** (1984) *A Handbook of Cognitive Psychology.* London: Lawrence Erlbaum Associates.

48 **Francis, H.** (1984) *Minds of their Own.* London University: Institute of Education.

49 **Fransson, A.** (1977) 'On qualitative differences in learning IV – Effects of motivation and test anxiety on process and outcome', *British Journal of Educational Psychology,* 47, 244–57.

50 **Friedlander, B. Z.** (1975) 'Some remarks on open education', *American Educational Research Journal,* 12, 465–8.

51 **Galton, M., Simon, B.** and **Croll, P.** (1980) *Inside the Primary School.* London: Routledge and Kegan Paul.

52 **Gardner, H.** (1984) *Frames of Mind.* London: Heinemann.

53 **Gardner, H.** (1985) 'The development and education of intelligences' in **Link, F.** (ed.) *Essays on the Intellect.* Washington DC: Curriculum Development Associates.

54 **Gibbs, G., Morgan, A.** and **Taylor, E.** (1984) 'The world of the learner' in **Marton, F., Hounsell, D. J.** and **Entwistle, N. J.** (eds) *The Experience of Learning.* Edinburgh: Scottish Academic Press.

55 **Godfrey Thomson Unit** (forthcoming) *Passage 10–13.* London: Hodder and Stoughton.

56 **Harré, R. M., Clarke, D.** and **De Carlo, N.** (1985) *Motives and Mechanisms.* London: Methuen.

57 **Hartley, R.** (1985) 'Using the computer for learning and teaching' in **Entwistle, N. J.** (ed.) *New Directions in Educational Psychology – Learning and Teaching.* Lewes: Falmer Press.

58 **Hodgson, V.** (1984) 'Learning from lectures' in **Marton F., Hounsell, D. J.** and **Entwistle, N. J.** (eds) *The Experience of Learning.* Edinburgh: Scottish Academic Press.

59 **Hudson, L.** (1966) *Contrary Imaginations.* London: Methuen.

60 **Kluckholm, C., Murray, H. A.** and **Schneider, D. M.** (1953) *Personality in Nature, Society and Culture.* New York: Knopf.

61 **Kogan, N.** (1976) *Cognitive Styles in Infancy and Early Childhood.* Hillsdale, NJ: Lawrence Erlbaum.

62 **Kozéki, B.** (1985) 'Motives and motivational styles in education' in **Entwistle, N. J.** (ed.) *New Directions in Educational Psychology – Learning and Teaching.* Lewes: Falmer Press.

63 **Laurillard, D.** (1984) 'Learning by problem solving' in **Marton, F., Hounsell, D. J.** and **Entwistle, N. J.** (eds) *The Experience of Learning.* Edinburgh: Scottish Academic Press.

64 **Leith, G. O. M.** (1974) 'Individual differences in learning interactions of personality and teaching methods' in *Personality and Academic Progress.* London: Association of Educational Psychologists.

65 **Marton, F.** (forthcoming) 'Phenomenography: a research approach to investigating different understandings of reality' in **Fetterman, D.** (ed.) *A Shift in Allegiance: the Use of Qualitative Data and its Relevance for Policy.*

66 **Marton, F., Hounsell, D. J.** and **Entwistle, N. J.** (1984) *The Experience of Learning.* Edinburgh: Scottish Academic Press.

67   **Messick, S.** (1976) *Individuality in Learning.* San Francisco: Jossey Bass.
68   **Mitchell, A.** (1985) *The Use of SCRIBE and SCOPE Computer Packages: Case Studies of Innovation in School-Based Assessment.* Edinburgh: Moray House College of Education.
69   **Neisser, U.** (1976) *Cognition and Reality.* San Francisco: Freeman.
70   **Nisbet, J. D.** and **Shucksmith, J.** (1986) *Learning Strategies.* London: Routledge and Kegan Paul.
71   **Norman, D. A.** and **Rumelhart, D. E.** (1975) *Explorations in Cognition.* San Francisco: Freeman.
72   **Novak, J. D.** and **Gowin, D. B.** (1984) *Learning How to Learn.* Cambridge: Cambridge University Press.
73   **Odor, J. P.** (1984) *Hard and Soft Technology for Education and Communication for Disabled People.* University of Edinburgh: CALL Centre, Department of Education.
74   **Odor, J. P., Pollitt, A. B.,** and **Entwistle, N. J.** (1986) *Item Banking: Developments and Potentialities.* University of Edinburgh: Godfrey Thomson Unit.
75   **O'Shea, T.** and **Self, J.** (1983) *Learning and Teaching with Computers.* Brighton: Harvester Press.
76   **Papert, S.** (1980) *Mindstorms: Children, Computers and Powerful Ideas.* New York: Basic Books.
77   **Pask, G.** (1976) 'Styles and strategies of learning', *British Journal of Educational Psychology*, 46, 128–48.
78   **Peel, E. A.** (1972) 'The quality of understanding in secondary school subjects', *Educational Review*, 24, 174–82.
79   **Piaget, J.** and **Inhelder, B.** (1969) *The Psychology of the Child.* London: Routledge and Kegan Paul.
80   **Pollitt, A. B., Hutchinson, C., Entwistle, N. J.** and **De Luca, C.** (1985) *What Makes Exam Questions Difficult?* Edinburgh: Scottish Academic Press.
81   **Pramling, I.** (1983) *The Child's Conception of Learning.* Gothenburg: Acta Universitatis Gothoburgensis.
82   **Ramsden, P.** (1981) 'A Study of the Relationship between Student Learning and its Academic Context', unpublished PhD thesis, University of Lancaster.
83   **Ramsden, P.** (1984) 'The context of learning' in **Marton, F., Hounsell, D. J.** and **Entwistle, N. J.** (eds) *The Experience of Learning.* Edinburgh: Scottish Academic Press.
84   **Resnick, L.** (1983) 'Toward a cognitive theory of instruction' in **Paris, S. G., Olson, G. M.** and **Stevenson, H. W.** (eds) *Learning and Motivation in the Classroom.* Hillsdale, NJ: Lawrence Erlbaum.
85   **Rogers, C. R.** (1961) *On Becoming a Person.* Boston: Houghton Mifflin.
86   **Rogers, C. R.** (1969) *Freedom to Learn.* Columbus, Ohio: Merrill.
87   **Rogers, C. R.** (1978) *Carl Rogers on Personal Power.* London: Constable.
88   **Rose, C.** (1985) *Accelerated Learning.* Great Missenden, Bucks: Topaz Publishing.
89   **Selmes, I. P.** (1985) 'Approaches to Learning at Secondary School: their Identification and Facilitation', unpublished PhD thesis, University of Edinburgh.
90   **Selmes, I. P.** (1987) *Improving Study Skills.* London: Hodder and Stoughton.
91   **Shayer, M.** and **Adey, P.** (1981) *Toward a Science of Science Teaching.* London: Heinemann.
92   **Skinner, B. F.** (1954) 'The science of learning and the art of teaching', *Harvard Educational Review*, 24, 86–97.
93   **Skinner, B. F.** (1968) *The Technology of Teaching.* New York: Appleton Century Crofts.

94 **Snow, R. E.** and **Lohman, D. F.** (1984) 'Toward a theory of cognitive aptitude for learning from instruction', *Journal of Educational Psychology*, 76, 347–76.

95 **Solomon, D.** and **Kendall, A. J.** (1979) *Children in Classrooms: an Investigation of Person-Environment Interaction*. New York: Praeger Publishers.

96 **Sperry, R.** (1983) *Science and Moral Priority*. Oxford: Blackwell.

97 **Sutherland, M.** (1985) 'Classroom interaction and sex differences', in **Bennett, S. N.** and **Desforges, C. W.** (eds) *Recent Advances in Classroom Research*. Edinburgh: Scottish Academic Press.

98 **Taylor, E.** (1983) 'Orientations to Study: A Longitudinal Interview Investigation of Students on Two Human Studies Degree Courses at Surrey University', unpublished PhD thesis, University of Surrey.

99 **Thomas, L.** and **Harri-Augstein, S.** (1985) *Self-Organised Learning*. London: Routledge and Kegan Paul.

100 **Tizard, J., Hewison, J.** and **Schofield, W.** (1985) 'Parental involvement and reading attainment', in **Entwistle, N. J.** (ed.) *New Directions in Educational Psychology – Learning and Teaching*. Lewes: Falmer Press.

101 **Trown, E. A.** and **Leith, G. O. M.** (1975) 'Decision rules for teaching strategies in primary schools: personality-treatment interactions', *British Journal of Educational Psychology*, 45, 130–40.

102 **Wade, B.** (1981) 'Highly anxious pupils in formal and informal primary classrooms: the relationship between inferred coping strategies and cognitive attainment', *British Journal of Educational Psychology*, 51, 39–49.

103 **Wheldall, K.** (1985) 'The use of behavioural ecology in classroom management', in **Entwistle, N. J.** (ed.) *New Directions in Educational Psychology – Learning and Teaching*. Lewes: Falmer Press.

Index

X